Friedrich Froebel

Friedrich Froebel

A Critical Introduction to Key Themes and Debates

TINA BRUCE

BLOOMSBURY ACADEMIC

LONDON • NEW YORK • OXFORD • NEW DELHI • SYDNEY

BLOOMSBURY ACADEMIC
Bloomsbury Publishing Plc
50 Bedford Square, London, WC1B 3DP, UK
1385 Broadway, New York, NY 10018, USA
29 Earlsfort Terrace, Dublin 2, Ireland

BLOOMSBURY, BLOOMSBURY ACADEMIC and the Diana logo are
trademarks of Bloomsbury Publishing Plc

First published in Great Britain 2021
Reprinted 2021

For legal purposes the Acknowledgements on p. x constitute an extension
of this copyright page.

Cover image: © Lausanne Project (Model), Gego (Goldschmidt, Gertrud Luise) /
Museo Nacional Centro de Arte Reina Sofía, Spain / with permission from Fundación
Gego, Venezuela

Bloomsbury Publishing Plc does not have any control over, or responsibility for, any
third-party websites referred to or in this book. All internet addresses given in this
book were correct at the time of going to press. The author and publisher regret any
inconvenience caused if addresses have changed or sites have ceased to exist, but can
accept no responsibility for any such changes.

A catalogue record for this book is available from the British Library.

Library of Congress Cataloging-in-Publication Data
Names: Bruce, Tina, author.
Title: Friedrich Froebel : a critical introduction to key themes and debates / Tina Bruce.
Description: London ; New York : Bloomsbury Academic, 2021. |
Includes bibliographical references and index.
Identifiers: LCCN 2020036932 (print) | LCCN 2020036933 (ebook) |
ISBN 9781474250436 (hardback) | ISBN 9781474250429 (paperback) |
ISBN 9781474250443 (ebook) | ISBN 9781474250450 (epub)
Subjects: LCSH: Fröbel, Friedrich, 1782–1852. |
Fröbel, Friedrich, 1782–1852–Influence. | Early childhood education–Philosophy.
Classification: LCC LB637 .B78 2021 (print) | LCC LB637 (ebook) |
DDC 372.21–dc23
LC record available at https://lccn.loc.gov/2020036932
LC ebook record available at https://lccn.loc.gov/2020036933

ISBN: HB: 978-1-4742-5043-6
PB: 978-1-4742-5042-9
ePDF: 978-1-4742-5044-3
eBook: 978-1-4742-5045-0

Typeset by Newgen KnowledgeWorks Pvt. Ltd., Chennai, India
Printed and bound in Great Britain

To find out more about our authors and books visit www.bloomsbury.com
and sign up for our newsletters.

Dedication

The day, 21 April, is a very important day in my life. It is the birthday of two people for whom I have the deepest respect. The first is Friedrich Froebel. The educational philosophy and approach of Froebel became central to my life when I was 18 years of age and his influence continues.

The second is my husband, Professor Ian Bruce CBE, who has empowered me for half a century now, and whose unfailing love and partnership in our shared commitment to family and our interwoven work has given me courage at times when this was needed, and great joy which brings a sense of fulfilment to our lives together.

The book is also dedicated to the Reconnecting Froebelians with whom I have had the pleasure of spending inspiring time in working together during the last decade. Together, as Froebelian communities, we are unearthing buried treasure through reconnecting Froebel's principles with his practices.

CONTENTS

FIGURES

NOTE ON THE AUTHOR

Tina Bruce CBE is an honorary professor of early childhood education at the University of Roehampton. She trained as a teacher for 3 to 13-year-olds at the Froebel Educational Institute, and studied for a postgraduate certificate in the education of children with profound and partial hearing impairment at the University of Manchester. She was the director of the Centre for Early Childhood Studies at the Froebel College. For ten years she was coordinator of the Early Years Ministerial Advisory Group. She is a vice president of Early Education, an associate member of the Froebel Trust and an executive committee member of the International Froebel Society. She is a Patron of the Centre for Literacy in Primary Education (CLPE).

ACKNOWLEDGEMENTS

My thanks to Yordanka Valkanova, who suggested that I should write this book and who introduced me to Rachel Eisenhauer at Bloomsbury Publishing. I would like to thank Bloomsbury Publishing (particularly Mark Richardson) for their kindness and understanding of the delay in the completion of this book when I was temporarily physically disabled, and the team, Zeba and Shyam, who have taken the book to the final publication.

The invaluable help I have received from Kerrie Curry who took the photographs and put together the illustrations and supported me in many other ways has saved me from feeling stressed and has made the work enjoyable. This is deeply appreciated and I thank her. As always, I have valued the support and encouragement of my family, my husband Ian, and from Hannah and Jonathan, Tom and Gemma.

I thank the Reconnected Froebelians I have the pleasure to work with, Sara Holroyd, Stella Louis and the team of Travelling Froebel Tutors, Sacha Powell, chief executive of the Froebel Trust, Jane Whinnett, co-chair of the Froebel Trust Education and Research Committee and Lynn McNair, Maureen Baker, Stella Brown, Catriona Gill, Chris McCormick of the Edinburgh Froebel Network, Jane Read. Working with colleagues in South Africa, Maggy Mdlada and Carole Bloch and in Western Australia with Libby Lee-Hammond has been a privilege. Thanks to Jane Read and Amy Palmer for the honour of including the oral history undertaken by Kate Hoskins and Sue Smedley in their book of Froebelian women. Also, thanks to Helen Tovey for introducing me to the work of Susan Herrington.

I should like to thank Elly Singer, Sandy Wong and Frances Press at the European Oral Histories Project at Charles Sturt University for inviting me to be interviewed to talk about Froebelian Play for *Chronicling the development of early childhood education and care since the 1970s -pedagogies and practices* (5 October 2018). The conversations with Elly, engaging with nature and children at play in Kew Gardens have felt like something I shall always treasure.

CHAPTER ONE

The Life and Historic Context of Friedrich Froebel

In this book, I advocate a *reconnection* of Froebelian principles with Froebelian practices. This requires a critical look at the key debates and challenges for Froebelians of today, wherever they work in the world. It is two centuries since Froebelian education began, and since then there have been waves of interpretations sweeping the field. Some Froebelians have taken his approach literally without deviation but, in doing so, have destroyed the spirit of what he tried to do. Others have kept what they liked and allowed the rest to fade or drop away. Those who have most influenced the interpretations of Froebel from the turn of the nineteenth century have, until recently, assimilated key aspects of his thinking into developments in other disciplines and theories, such as psychology, sociology, neuroscience and postmodern thinking. In doing so, they disconnected the principles and, in effect, outlawed the practice, suggesting it to be obsolete. It is time to reconnect Froebelian principles and practices and, in doing so, unearth buried treasure. Reconnection with Froebel means looking at his work as an interconnected whole, and not in fragmented pieces. Separating principles from practice destroys his vision of *Unity*. Reconnectors are Froebelians who are trying to work with the whole Froebelian framework.

This chapter begins with a timeline to support readers as they journey through the book.

It outlines descriptively the key events in Froebel's life and gives the historical and cultural context in which he lived. This is not undertaken in a strictly linear way, working instead on gathering together emergent points in his thinking, how these developed and then came to fruition.

1782–92

Friedrich Wilhelm August Froebel was born, on 21 April, in Oberweissbach in the Thuringian Forest (Germany) (Figure 1.1). He was the youngest child with five older siblings: August (born 1766), Christoph (born 1768), Christian (born 1770), Juliane (born 1774) and Traugott (born 1778). His mother, Jakobine died when he was 10 months old. His father, Jakob Froebel, was a strict Lutheran pastor who spent little time with his sons, who were looked after by servants. He adhered to a literal understanding of the Bible and emphasized his belief in Hell. His father remarried two years after the death of his wife. Froebel's stepmother at first showered him with loving care but, when she gave birth to her first child, she became neglectful of him and gradually came to reject him. He became close to his 14-year-old brother Christoph until he went to university to study theology and only came home during the holidays. He spent his time alone in the garden and in the attic. He attended the girl's school opposite the house between the ages of 7 to 10.

1793–6

At the age of 10, he went to live with his maternal uncle who was a gentler and kinder Lutheran pastor than his father. His uncle had recently lost his wife and son. Froebel felt nurtured in this more affectionate home. He met and went to school with other boys of his age, with whom he played and went into the countryside, appreciating the freedom in this. The contrast between the two homes was felt in deep and permanent ways by Froebel. He had experienced what it felt like to be in a dysfunctional family context. He had also experienced the nurture and well-being of living in a loving and affectionate home, in which he was allowed to ask questions and to develop his own thoughts without being judged and punished. He began to tease out the difference between the God of his father's faith and the loving God of his uncle's Christianity.

1797–1800

Froebel left school and his uncle's home when he was 15 years old. Having spent long hours in the garden in his younger days and later exploring the countryside with his school friends when living with his uncle, he had developed a deep love of and *Engagement with Nature*. He was also good at mathematics. He was apprenticed for three years to a forester but was given little tuition and so, once again, found himself spending long hours alone.

However, he used the access he was given to the library to take the time to learn about botany, using books which helped him to classify the trees and plants he found in the forest. These experiences gave him opportunities to think about what the laws of nature might be. His emergent thinking about the concept of *Unity* began. Because of his loneliness he asked to leave the apprenticeship before the three years were completed, which made his father angry. With the support from Froebel's siblings, his father finally gave permission for Froebel to use the small legacy his mother had left him to finance a place at the University of Jena, where his brother Traugott was studying.

At Jena he soon realized that his lack of education had not prepared him for this level of study of botany and mathematics. He began to see the need to study these subjects in a more integrated way. His botany tutor, August Johann Georg Karl Batsch, was helpful and encouraged him to see interconnections and unity in nature. He yearned for a more holistic approach to knowledge. He found himself lacking in friends, inexperienced as he was in the kind of socializing that he found at the university. He lent his older brother Traugott money, which he failed to repay in time for Froebel to pay his own bills. Consequently, Froebel was sent to the debtor's prison for two months until released when his furious father paid off his bill.

1801–4

He considered emigrating to America or Russia to avoid the wrath he experienced from his father. However, his father became ill that year and Froebel returned home to help in the parish. They became more appreciative of each other in working together until his father died in 1802. Froebel felt it was a redemptive experience. He then left home, staying in touch with his brother Christoph. He became, through a series of different kinds of work, a bursar, land surveyor and farm manager in both south and north Germany until he made the decision that he would like to become an architect. He paid for his studies in the liberal city of Frankfurt by teaching in a school where the head of the Experimental School (Liebschner, 2001), Anton Gruner had been trained by Johann Heinrich Pestalozzi and soon invited him to teach in the school. Froebel taught a class of forty boys. He fell in love with teaching. He wanted to visit Pestalozzi's training school in Yverdun in Switzerland but could not afford to do so then.

1805–7

During the summer holidays he was able to make this visit, financed by Frau Caroline von Holzhausen whose sons he tutored. He came to see her as an idealized mother. He sent her reports of his visit to Pestalozzi's school. On his return he taught for a short time at the Experimental School again but then he became the full-time tutor of the two sons of Frau von Holzhausen. The marriage was an unhappy one. With tension between the parents growing, and Froebel's deepening feelings for Frau Caroline, Froebel readily and wisely agreed and promoted the idea that the boys should go with him to Pestalozzi's school to study.

1808–11

Froebel arrived in Yverdun at the historical point when Pestalozzi's work was at its height and was much studied and visited by educators from different countries. However, he began to find that his thinking differed in quite fundamental ways. Froebel focused on the potential that he saw in children, especially the young children. Pestalozzi, he felt, saw them as they were at the time, rather than seeing what they might become. Froebel was influenced in the view he took by the thinking of the Silesian seventeenth-century thinker Jacob Boehme (Smith, 1983: 307). This led him to see life (with education being a part of life) as a process of becoming, so that change was embedded in living. He parted from Pestalozzi on good terms and Froebel always afterwards acknowledged the huge help the experience of spending time in Pestalozzi's school had been in forming his approach to education. For example, he valued the emphasis on the use of real objects – the 'object lesson' – although he felt that the context of the objects should be given more place in the experience. He learnt the importance of observation, which was invaluable in his later work, and the skills he developed in this contributed in deep ways to his recognition of the educational need for young children to play. Pestalozzi recognized the importance of family in early childhood. Getting to know the ideas, thoughts, feelings and relationships of the baby, toddler or child was, Froebel gradually realized, at the heart of teaching. He gave a place to education as part of a nurturing environment from birth. During early childhood, babies, toddlers and young children are already experiencing life. They are not preparing for life. They are alive. Froebel therefore believed that at each age, education is part of life, and that this is so throughout life. His later book *The Mother Play and Nursery Songs* (1844) developed his thinking about the importance of home as part of the process of becoming, which continues during the whole of life. He was, he always acknowledged, deeply influenced by the time he spent in Pestalozzi's school.

He returned with the two sons of Caroline von Holzhausen to continue as their tutor but soon left to study at the University of Gottingen because of his deepening relationship with their mother. It is possible that her son, born soon afterwards, was Froebel's, although there was possibly a reconciliation in her marriage at that time. It is more likely that Froebel felt he must leave, given that this was so. They continued to write to each other until 1816, and without doubt she influenced his belief that women were able to be good teachers and educators.

1812

He soon left the University of Gottingen to work on crystallography at the invitation of Professor Weiss at Berlin University. This was the cutting-edge science of the time, signalling the emergence of chemistry as a new discipline. It was during this time that, in a restless state having taken the decision that he must leave the company of Caroline von Holzhausen, he developed his *spherical law* involving the *law of opposites*. This was part of his quest to find the laws of nature. This led to his developing the concept of *Unity,* with the interconnectivity of the inner and the outer, the *law of opposites*, the awareness of the self in relationship with community and nature, and for Froebel, with God.

1813

Froebel joined the army in the fight against Napoleon, but never saw battle. He met two fellow students from Berlin, Wilhelm Middendorff and Heinrich Langethal, who proved to be very important in his life and became central figures in the founding and development of the school in Keilhau.

1814

With the coming of peace, he became the scientific assistant at the Mineralogical museum in Berlin and, two years later, the curator of the museum in Stockholm pursuing his interest in crystallography which was driven by his longing to find the laws of nature.

1817–18

His brother Christoph died, leaving three young children and his widow. Their family home in Griesheim was the nucleus of his first school. His brother Christian sent his two sons to the school and so the numbers grew. Middendorff came to help (eventually taking over the school after Froebel's death in 1852). Langethal's younger brother joined them. A small farm was bought, funded by Christoph's wife, in Keilhau and by 1820 the school community numbered fifty-six. Langethal joined the group to help with the teaching. From the beginning, the emphasis in the school was to help children think for themselves rather than to receive knowledge from the teacher. Middendorff and Langethal formed a crucial part of what became a stable, loyal and committed core team. These then included Froebel's first wife Wilhelmine Henriette Hoffmeister, and after her death, Luise Leven his second wife. Wilhelmine Henriette's foster daughter Ernestine Crispini married Langethal. Middendorff married Albertine, the oldest daughter of Froebel's older brother Christian. Middendorff's nephew, Johannes Barop, married Christian's second daughter, Emilie, soon after joining the Keilhau community in 1828. This group, and others who were part of it, are the reason why his work came to fruition. He (and they) understood, over the years, the importance of working together as a community. They supported Froebel's work, despite his lack of skill in dealing with management and finances, and they dealt with his unusual but creative and inspirational ways of working, which did not lead to easy lives for any of them.

Froebel had married Henriette Wilhelmine in 1818. She was the daughter of an aristocrat who opposed the marriage. She had divorced an abusive husband and could not have children because of the violence she had endured in her marriage. They were together until her death in 1839 in a very harmonious and respectful relationship. She supported his work and contributed to it quietly, especially in the developing of the work that led to the founding of the Blankenburg Kindergarten and the development of the *Gifts* which arose from Froebel's observation of the needs of young children to play. She also quietly helped him in his work leading to the *Mother Songs*.

1824

The Prussian government feared that the school in Keilhau was a bed of revolution and atheism and instigated an inspection. Fortuitously this resulted in a glowing report from the experienced and respected inspector.

1826

The glowing inspection report eased the way to the publication of *The Education of Man*, which documents the first years of the school in Keilhau.

1827

The Prussian government decreed that children must be educated in the state schools. As a result, numbers in the Keilhau school decreased from sixty to five children. The school was saved from collapse because the builders and craftsmen who had made the expanded school did not pursue collecting their debts. It was typical of Froebel to face times of difficulty by intense planning on his vision of education. Perhaps this saved him from a state of despair. He developed the Helba Plan at the request of the Duke of Meiningen for a school, which was not carried forward. This outlined an inclusive approach from the earliest age where children of different backgrounds and religions, especially the Jewish families of colleagues and friends, would learn together, building on the individual strengths and character of each child.

1828–35

Johannes Barop arrived to teach at Keilhau and proved to be an invaluable addition to the core team. As soon as he joined the community, he reassured anxious parents and improved the school image by dealing with the financial situation. After Froebel's death in 1852, Middendorff became head and was succeeded on his death by Barop.

Between 1828 and 1836 several schools were set up in Switzerland, with Middendorff, Barop and Langethal helping in different ways to deal with opposition which was suggesting that the schools were beds of revolution and irreligious.

Froebel had been interested in the play of young children from his days while working with Pestalozzi, and devoted more time to observing and pondering the value and reasons why young children seem to need to engage in it. When asked to help with education in the Burgdorf orphanage, he began designing the *Gifts* (six sets of wooden blocks) with the help of his wife Wilhelmine Henriette, writing about this in *Early Childhood Pedagogics*.

1836

Froebel and Wilhelmine Henriette moved to Blankenburg and in a large, empty space began organizing the making of what became known as the *Gifts* and *Occupations*. The teachers they worked with would carry these boxes of wooden blocks with them wherever they went.

1838

Through one of the staff at Keilhau, Frankenberg, Froebel was invited to Dresden to present a demonstration attended by the queen, who showed great interest in it. His wife was unable to attend because of her deteriorating health, but Wilhelmine Henriette died knowing that the work she had helped him with was becoming recognized.

1840

He invented the name Kindergarten to describe his school for the youngest children which was opened on 28 June 1840 in Blankenburg with the encouragement of the city fathers who made him an Honorary Citizen of the town.

1844

This year saw the publication of the *Mother Play and Nursery Songs (Mutter und Koselieder)*. After this publication, he turned his attention to the education of women. His thoughts had been forming since 1839, when he wrote a letter to 'The Women of Blankenburg' in which he invited them to form women's associations where they would be able to discuss the education of Kindergarten children. He had found mothers to be very interested in developing the learning of their children. He spoke at a conference for teachers, head teachers, university staff including professors and ministers of education. He put forward his belief that women, who represent half of humanity, should be able to train to teach children. The audience, all men, burst into laughter.

1847

Froebel returned to Keilhau determined to train women Kindergarten teachers, including Henriette Breyman his grandniece. She later became founder of the Pestalozzi-Froebel House in Hamburg. Another Keilhau-trained Kindergarten teacher was Luise Levin, who became his wife in 1851.

1848

He accepted the invitation of the Duke of Meiningen to set up an Institute for all embracing Life-Unity in one of his castles where there was to be a Kindergarten, an orphanage, a training college for Kindergarten teachers, opportunities for men and women to develop arts and crafts, a school for boys and girls to university level and a centre developing educational materials for children. Only the training college and Kindergarten were established while the castle was being prepared and this work began, until 1850, in nearby Liebenstein in 1849 with eight students. Frau von Marenholtz-Bulow and Frau Johanna Goldschmidt (nee Swabe) saw the work and became committed lifelong supporters of Froebelian education.

1851

A Verbot issued by the Prussian government decreed that all Kindergartens must close. This was following the involvement of Froebel's nephews, Julius in socialist activity and his brother Karl's writing advocating in a socialist manner the education for women when head of the High School for Women in Hamburg. Froebel took unprecedented action and wrote to the king of Prussia dissociating himself from Karl and requesting a public inquiry into the work of the Kindergartens. No public inquiry followed, but two important conferences took place. The first was in Liebenstein attended by supporters of Froebel including the Minister of State of Weimar. At the second, in 1852 in Gotha, Froebel received a standing ovation honouring his work. He fell ill soon after and died on 21 June.

Family

Visiting the birth place of Froebel, now a museum, in the small town of Oberweissbach in Thuringia, foregrounds the hugely dominant influence of the church that his father, the strict and stern Lutheran minister, raised funds from his parishioners to build in 1779. This was achieved at crippling expense to the congregation, and the church still needs constant repairs and maintenance today as a leaflet given out to visitors demonstrates. The church is of vast dimension given the geographical area and the small population. It is referred to as the Cathedral of South Thuringia. Froebel's mother, Jakobine, is buried in the churchyard at the back of the house. It is perhaps significant that Froebel's father was buried next to her when he died, despite having been married a second time. Because of his father's sternness and his stepmother's rejection of him, from an early age Froebel retreated to the attic and spent lonely times in the garden where he became an acute and active observer of nature. In the attic there are still herbs hanging on the rafters to dry. Froebel learnt about the cultivation of herbs with his father, as this was an important part of the traditional trade in this part of Germany. Learning about growing and cultivating herbs with his father was one of the happiest parts of his childhood (Community Playthings, 2016:10). His close relationship with his brother Christoph, who was 14 years older was also important to him and later Froebel created the first school in Griesheim, the home of his widow and children. Love lasts, and the love Christoph had

FIGURE 1.1 Friedrich Froebel 1782–1852.

given him as a little boy continued after his death. Froebel's love of Caroline von Holzhausen, whose sons he tutored, remained and influenced his belief that women should be offered opportunities to train as Kindergarten teachers, leading to the foundation of the first training college for women.

There are deeply significant themes of the Froebelian educational approach in formation here, and they open up the debates about Froebelian education which have been revisited repeatedly since he opened his first school in Griesheim in 1817. It is important to emphasize that as a child Froebel felt safe and protected from the harsh discipline and inflexible rules of the house when he spent time in the attic, with its cosy corners and the possibility of peeping out of the dormer windows. Later, in the school he pioneered, planned and saw built in Keilhau (1817), he put into his architecture small, cosy hideaway areas in which children still find and enjoy the personal space this offers. The building he later pioneered in Keilhau attests to his being an imaginative architect, with the children he was building for at the centre. Den building in the school garden is still a feature of Froebelian education, and when it takes place in the garden it tends to be more often social than solitary. Children often build dens together and visit each other's creations. This had not been so for Froebel, who did not meet many other children until he attended school. Extraordinarily, he was then sent to the school for girls across the road from his house. This was reputed to have a higher academic standard than the school for boys which was next to it. He was not permitted to attend the services at his father's church, and so spent time alone in the vestry, perhaps being able to hear the sermon and the music floating out from within and the sound of the church bell tolling.

Froebel found the garden to be a place where there is beauty, peace and tranquillity. But the garden was also a functional experience during his childhood. This is because it provided the opportunity to learn about the everyday traditional work of people living in the Oberweissbach area. In this region of Germany local people still make oils and ointments. Classes are taught about the tradition plants and ointments in the house (now a museum) where Froebel was born and spent his early childhood. The practical know-how which Froebel acquired, in relation to learning about the importance of the function of plants as well as the beauty of a garden, became integrated with a depth of knowledge and understanding of nature. *Engagement with Nature* is of great importance in Froebelian education. Froebel's experience in the garden was perhaps a rehearsal of his life long search for *Unity*, which he found in the laws of nature and its interconnectivity.

Evelyn Lawrence was the director of the National Froebel Foundation. She considers how the 'wistful contemplation of other, happier homes, led to the idealisation of the role of the mother, and to a realisation of the paramount importance of the mother-child relationship in the development of every human being' (1952:3). There is probably in this an integration of Enlightenment and Romanticism. This will be explored in greater depth in Chapter Five of the book, when the nuanced layers surrounding the *Mother Songs* and *Finger Plays* are reflected upon and analysed. It is further illuminated in Chapter Eight when the importance of family and community are highlighted.

Froebel felt the importance of giving children the possibility of feeling safe from loneliness and isolation. The family emerges as having an
important role in this, and the importance of nurture, affection and love
has a central place. The contribution of women is valued. The creation
of mitigating and healing resources, through architecture with nooks and
crannies with safe corners and den building in gardens are given a place.
The power of nature to engage, support and extend the whole physical,
emotional and the intellectual life which is there from the beginning. That
intellectual life is part of the physical and emotional learning is education in its full sense. The social element of love and nurture is also part
of this. In early life, it is yearned for. In his educational approach, it has a
central place.

The gradual decision to become an educator

It took some years before Froebel found himself as an educator. People
do not immediately know what they wish to become. Until that time, his
search for the laws of nature, the unity and interconnectedness in science
and in the world as a whole stood him in good stead for his later work on
education. It made him robust in facing the onslaught of challenges that
his approach to education met consistently. It was a typical response to
the potential destruction of his work in 1827 to create the imaginative but
unfulfilled Helba Plan. Staying true to a vision, in this case of how education
might change and grow, is a characteristic feature of good leaders. Helping
children to think is still not a popular message in many educational settings
across the world. Preparing them to be compliant members of the workforce
is favoured more.

Froebel's sense of moral duty to strive for better ways of educating children, particularly babies, toddlers and young children, was unfailing and
relentless once he had made the decision to devote himself to education.

Forming communities of practice, such as Keilhau, is a powerful way of
working together. The professional training of Kindergarten teachers in a
small community is a powerful experience, which has lasting influence on
the future work undertaken by those trained in this way. Communities of
practice involve teamwork even when the staff do not live on the premises.
Feeling part of a community strengthens educational practice, according to
the Froebelian tradition. Froebel valued this deeply. He saw it as essential
to develop close-knit communities of Froebelian practice through which to
reflect, challenge themselves and debate together from a shared perspective. Froebel had experienced the way that the school Pestalozzi founded
got into difficulty. Disagreements about the way education in the school
should develop was a warning to Froebel. It showed that when freedom
of ideas and encouragement to debate and discuss are encouraged without

leadership, fragmentation is likely. Sustaining the foundational vision, while developing it so that ossification does not set in, is a matter of the utmost urgency. Very few leaders can achieve this in practice. Dealing with disagreements is part of this process. The team around Froebel worked with him in ways which brought this about and their contribution and participation in this process of becoming cannot be underestimated.

An approach embracing inclusion and diversity in a context which is conservative and supportive of the status quo, or even hostile to its ideals, became a major challenge for Froebel's work. At the end of his life his Kindergarten schools in Saxony were closed and banned through the Verbot in 1851. There is tragedy in that Froebel died in 1852. It might appear that the authority of powerful authoritarian and repressive politics prevailed. But did it? The banning of Froebelian education caused committed Froebelians to leave Saxony and take his work to different parts of the world where it flourished and took root, becoming

> the kindergarten journey from Bad Blankenburg in the 1840s, across oceans, continents, cultures and centuries, to the furthest outpost of kindergarten colonial endeavour ... Yet amidst the relocation and adaptation, some enduring Froebelian metaphors of kindergarten pedagogy and practice are evident.
>
> (May, 2017:167–8)

Becoming committed to the education of young children

The search for *Unity* was a long journey and continued throughout Froebel's life as part of the educational process of becoming. It anchored him in the face of opposition and gave him strength in staying true to his vision of education and life as being interconnected. He benefitted from the empowerment of being part of a community of like-minded people, and this gave him the ability to be robust in coming and going from it in order to deal with the issues facing his thinking in the world beyond. Great leaders are not afraid to surround themselves with brilliant people. Both being part of and looking beyond the community makes the spread of ideas more likely.

> There was nothing solitary about the enlightened ones of the eighteenth century. It is one thing to think *for* yourself, another to think *by* yourself, and the enlightened ones were not much given to thinking by themselves. On the contrary, thinking was regarded as an essentially social activity. People thought with each other; that is, they *shared* their thoughts.
>
> (Broadie, 2007:20, emphasis in the original)

It is certainly the case that the first wave of Kindergartners had met and trained with Froebel. But with the Verbot causing a considerable proportion to leave Germany, Froebelian supporters like Baroness von Marenholz-Bulow spread the ideas to others and so a second wave of Froebelian interpretations emerged. The Unitarian Julia Salis-Schwabe, who was a generous funder and founder of the Froebel Educational Institute in London, was one of these. She

> came to see Froebel's philosophy, with its practical system for developing the physical, mental and moral powers in children as the key to social progress.
>
> (Weston, 2002:5)

Unravelling the writings of Froebel

There are several reasons why Froebel's writing is hard to unravel. Froebel's writings are non-linear and badly structured. He was not confident of his ability to write well and felt that his education had not prepared him to achieve a high level of writing. An additional consideration is that his thinking is nuanced. Engaging with the layers of his thinking is both practically necessary and intellectually challenging. This is partly because the subsequent translation from German into English is a factor. But there are also unfortunate aspects to his image today in that the publisher, Hailmann, who brought the first translation of his work from German to English, would not agree to the title being presented as *The Education of Humanity*, which would have been the correct wording. He felt that this would not sell. The book was therefore given what now has a connotation of being a sexist title *The Education of Man*. This is an unfortunate legacy. In some ways Froebel can be given this label. His writings and the illustrations in the book of *Mother Play and Nursery Songs* reveal that he referred more to boys. He certainly saw the roles of men and women as different, but his recognition that women are capable of making a major contribution to society and to take on professional training and work in doing so shows that he was not sexist. It is a fact that until the 1990s, in most educational texts in the English language, children were still referred to as 'he', so perhaps it is more important to bear in mind the historic era and cultural context in which educationalists are operating than to automatically judge past educators according to current ways of thinking. The important thing is to decide whether the work pioneered by Froebel is rendered obsolete and therefore needing to be discarded, or whether his values about children and women can be transformed into current educational contexts in ways which remain useful today.

Unravelling what he really thought through an academic examination of his writings, both in the early days of his work and towards the end of his life, is fortunately only one way of coming to understand Froebel. Another way to throw light on what a Froebelian educational framework consists of is to see how those who worked with him at first hand used his educational philosophy and framework. Froebel was a doer, who could demonstrate and bring about what he strived for in educating children and working closely with their families. Those who worked closely with him constantly begged him to set down with clarity his educational ideas and reasoning. He realized that setting things engraved in stone was not a good idea. Unfortunately, those who followed in his footsteps after his death often wrote about the Froebelian approach in ways which resulted in the practice being narrow. Ossification set in, with its inevitable aridity and prescriptive consequences (Ronge and Ronge, 1855).

Spending time with a good teacher is far more helpful and effective than studying the theory in a book or being instructed through a lecture. A key to good teaching is: first to actively observe a Froebelian teacher; then be supported in trying out the practice; and then to reflect together, followed by reading on the subject and putting together thoughts with written reflections. The definition of teaching by the author of this book is 'observe, support, extend' (Bruce, 1987:65). This applies to student teachers as much as it does to the children being taught. It chimes with Froebel's thinking. Teachers learn to be teachers through the practical context of teaching with those who are good at it. They do, however, and this was something which Froebel believed deeply, need to be highly educated, avid readers and mature in order to develop their practice maximally. With experience, they might also write about it in published forms, but this has never, until recent years, been a highly developed part of the Froebelian tradition (Bruce, 2020).

Froebel was, by all accounts, an inspiring and outstanding teacher and surrounded himself with a brilliant group of colleagues who shared his values and were committed to his educational ideas. They became a strong group of practising tutors who could train others in the Froebelian approach. They took their Froebelian training with them and shared it, founding Kindergartens in different parts of the world. But the same issues emerge wherever Froebelian education is practised. This is as true today as it was in 1852. The only difference is that now there is no one who worked with or trained directly with Froebel. Dealing with disagreements among themselves about what a Kindergarten education should be and how true it is to Froebel's vision is one issue. External challenges brought about through sustained funding streams, official regulations and laws concerning the education of children in different parts of the world is another. These two themes of challenge continue in the transgobal arena.

The difficulties Froebel experienced, in setting down in written form his philosophy of education, are apparent in his books but are less of a problem in his regular journal newsletters or his private letters, in which he is more relaxed. The need for translation from German is a challenge, together with the different historic time and culture in which he operated.

G. Dahlberg, P. Moss and A. Pence ([1999]2013:30) suggest that we need to be alert to the way in which what is seen as knowledge begins to shape our thinking, such that it becomes normalized but is really only our understanding of what we think knowledge is. This makes an important point and is certainly what followed after Froebel's death. (Bruce in Bruce, Elfer and Powell, 2019:4–7). In attempts to stay close to Froebelian practice, as it was understood to be, the practice and the training of practitioners often became ossified and prescriptive. People stopped thinking in the sense of the mature reasoning which Immanuel Kant (1781) advocates and which Michael Foucault (1980:131) later articulated as essential if 'regimes of truth' are to be curbed from taking over. The challenges to Froebel's vision of a community of practice need to be born in mind and acted on in implementation.

The political and cultural context

While studying at Jena, Froebel came into contact with the ideas of the philosophers – Johann Fichte (1762–1814) who advocated bowing to authority, and Georg Wilhelm Friedrich Hegel (1770–1831) – who 'developed a method based on dialectical resolution of opposites that would lead to beauty in the perceptual realm' (Brosterman, 1997:114). It was not long since the publication of Kant's *Critique of Pure Reason* (1781) who emphasized the development of a sense of public and moral duty. Jean Jacques Rousseau's thinking, and his book *Emile*, published in 1762, was much under discussion at this time. He argued that human beings are naturally good. This was seen as a revolutionary attack on the Christian notion of original sin. Rousseau influenced Pestalozzi who emphasized intrinsic motivation, the importance of observation, active physical learning and nature walks rather than book learning.

> Froebel was in due course to build on and develop Rousseau's proposal and Pestalozzi's practice with more systematic theoretical rigour, based partly on a unique combination of his reading in idealist philosophy, partly in his early and solitary interaction with nature in the woods around his home and partly on his later studies in crystallography and science that was entering an exciting period of development'.
>
> (Weston, 1998:7)

He was conscious of the influence of Pestalozzi on his thinking, and Christian Samuel Weiss who taught him crystallography but although he attended lectures given by Fichte, Froebel took a different view of authority and even though the *law of opposites* became central to Froebel's concept of *Unity* it did not appear to come to him from Hegel except by the process of osmosis with his dialectical thinking being, metaphorically speaking, in the air in Jena at that time.

> The early nineteenth century was a turbulent period in Europe, both intellectually, as some of the greatest names in world philosophy were writing and teaching in the universities where Froebel studied, and politically, as Napoleonic imperialism defeated the apparently invincible Prussia and cleared the way for German Nationalism.
>
> (Weston, 1998:1)

Another influence which was part of the times was the developing German nationalism. Napoleon had eroded the multitude of dukedoms and there was a movement towards the unification of Germany to become one republican state. Froebel's developing concept of *Unity* and his contact with German nationalists such as Ernst Arndt (1769–1860) in Jena and the Halle Burschenschaft student association may well have led him to name the Griesham school (1817) the *Universal German Educational Institute*. It is not therefore surprising that his schools and Kindergartens were perceived by the king of Prussia to be hotbeds of atheism and revolution. Education was seen as a mechanism through which to bring about social change. It was therefore something which alarmed those in power in Prussia at the time.

In 1851, when the Verbot was issued, Froebel's Kindergartens were banned. J. Liebschner ([1992]2001) reports that despite two conferences – the first of which, at Liebenstien in 1851, included the supportive attendance of the Minister of State for Weinmar and another conference in 1852 in Gotha when he arrived late to be greeted with a standing ovation, honouring him as the leading educator in Germany – Froebel's schools in Saxony continued to be banned. The Kindergarten Verbot in 1851, the year before his death, asserted that Froebelian Kindergartens preached revolution and undermined religion. It was unfortunate that Froebel's nephews, Julius and Karl, (the sons of his brothers Christoph and Christian) who had attended the school in Keilhau, were involved in the publication of pamphlets promoting material such as the importance of education for women. Education that took a liberal form and encouraged thinking was viewed with anxiety by the state. To open up further opportunities for the education of people was a grave matter. In addition, Marion Smith writes that, 'His statements about religion were sometimes both contradictory and obscure and can easily give foundation to changes of heresy and pantheism.' (1983:307). With the state of affairs in Prussia at this historic time both church and state quashed independent and liberal thought. The Verbot was not lifted until 1860, which was eight years after his death.

There is a difference between the revolutionary discarding of traditional authority and engaging in a thoughtful consideration of practices handed down and examining these so that practice changes because it needs to, rather than because it must. In this respect it is perhaps significant that

Froebel was skilled in gaining the support of generous funders, like the Duke of Meiningen, in setting up his schools and the training college. He brought with him influential people, like Baroness von Marenholtz-Bulow at key points in the development of his work. Those who opposed him were threatened by him and they held the power. This resulted in the imposition of inspections, regulations undermining the schools and the Verbot. But in the long term, Froebel's approach to education has survived and just as in Froebel's day when inspections take place, the quality of education is found to be high. Why does it not receive more encouragement from the politicians who hold the power? Perhaps, just as in Froebel's time, there is fear of encouraging children to be educated to think. The intellectual life that has thoughtful feelings and a moral framework remains threatening.

The philosopher David Aspin is both critical and praising of Froebel, taking the view that 'along with much that was dross in his theory, there is much than can be regarded as gold' (1983:265). He argues that his thinking is in important respects 'profoundly modern' (Aspin, 1983:268). Aspin draws on the work of the philosopher T. W. Moore (1974), who suggests that any educational theory should contain a theory of knowledge, a philosophy of mind and a set of moral values and a metaphysical basis:

He (*Froebel*) advances, under a highly dubious metaphysic, and ethics of education that is at the least contentious: at the same time his work reconciles under one head, so many disparate elements that we can see in his theory one harmonious whole, that has conjoined and systematised all the aspects that Moore differentiates as the discrete parts of any educational theory.

(Aspin, 1983:271)

CHAPTER TWO

The Whole Child and the Concept of *Unity*

Froebel believed that everything in the universe is linked. This interconnectivity is one of the most important features of the Froebelian educational approach. This is why it is analysed this early on in the book, following the need to situate Froebel in the key events and context of his life in the first chapter. The child

> attains both a general knowledge of the whole and an insight into the parts, so that his memory is impressed simultaneously with relations of place, object, name, qualities and time (through noting the various stages of development of the plant) and combines them. (Welton, 1912:240–1)

Throughout his life, beginning in the garden where he spent so much time as a child, Froebel sought what he described as the laws of nature. This search continued when he left school to become apprenticed to a forester, while studying mathematics, botany and other subjects at the university, crystallography at the Berlin museum and later as an educator, when he established his schools, invented the Kindergarten and created what was probably the first teacher training college for women:

> It was during the two years of daily work with crystals that Froebel's two major interests, nature and education, finally intersected in a cohesive and easily demonstrable fashion that would result, many years later, in the creation of the first kindergarten. (Brosterman, 1997:25)

The searching for the laws which bring about interconnectivity in the universe and between communities of people, and the connections within left him in a very unsettled state, with a restlessness that lasted throughout his life. He wanted to understand how the *inner* becomes *outer* and the *outer* becomes *inner*. He was fascinated by what he came to call the *law of opposites* as part of this journey. He consistently, and in a very sustained way throughout his life, puzzled over and pondered the relationships, connections and links between knowing yourself, but knowing yourself in relationship with and through others, the wider world and the universe itself. He calls this the *spherical law*:

> He assumed that there is something in man which is of the same nature as God; that the universe represents an aspect of God; that therefore all are, in some sense, one, and that there is a constant striving between opposites.
>
> (Smith, 1983:308)

A childhood experiencing two versions of a Christian God

During Froebel's childhood, he experienced two entirely different Christian gods. The first Christian religion he encountered was a God of hellfire and original sin, and hard to please, so that the young child was left feeling he could never be good. In his *Autobiography of Friedrich Froebel,* he writes that it was a great joy to him when he 'proved completely to my own satisfaction that I was not destined to go to hell' (Froebel, [1886]1915:11). The second version of the Christian religion, he met was a God who was loving. Both his father and his maternal uncle were Lutheran pastors, as outlined in Chapter One. They gave Froebel entirely different experiences of religion. But the hellfire experience came first, and lasted for ten years or so and was alongside the loss of his mother together with the harshness of his stepmother.

It is perhaps no wonder that consequently, as a young man and throughout his life, Froebel had an inner driving need to find a different God who was nevertheless Christian. He never rejected Christianity. Perhaps this was influenced by his older brother Christoph with whom he was the closest, who studied theology at the university. According to Marion Smith (1983:303–4) Christoph would return from the university during holidays and debate on religion with their stern father. Froebel began to see that there were differences of view, and this probably contributed to his feeling that what his father held as true in Christian religious belief and practice was not the only way. In addition, following a visit to Oberweissbach, when he could see how unhappy his late sister's son was, his maternal uncle gave him a home full of affection and love with deeply held moral values which showed a different Christian religion in practice.

Had he been born in a different culture or period in history, Froebel may have teased out the concept of *Unity* that he came to believe was in all things in a different way. But the essence of his findings is helpful to those who do not find themselves led to a divinity which is a core part of the Christian tradition:

> Rather than a redeemer of sinners, Jesus is seen as epitomising the perfect, fully lived life, the example which, internalized, provides the ideal of one's self to which the fully human life can aspire.
>
> (Best, 2016:5)

This gives another lens through which to see his commitment to the relationship between the *inner* and the *outer*, which is so central to his concept of *Unity*. What matters is the way that values are internalized, and not just paying lip service externally. This has contributed to the development of Froebelian approaches to education in different parts of the world and in different cultural contexts. There is an openness and flexibility in the way in which Froebel attempts to grapple with what constitute the laws of self, life and the nature of the universe:

> To make the internal external and the external internal, to find the unity for both, this is the general external form in which their destiny is expressed. Therefore, every external object comes to man with the invitation to determine its nature and relationships. For this he has his senses, the organs that enable him to meet the invitation. (Froebel, 1897:41)

Can non-Christians be Froebelians?

I am a freethinker, who does not believe in the existence of a God/gods. The early Froebelians, pioneering Froebelian principles and implementing them in practice in the UK context at the turn of the nineteenth to the twentieth century, were often Unitarians:

> Unitarians believed that social evils were the result of human action, not of original sin, and therefore that they could be remedied by human effort. (Weston, 2002:5)

An example is Julia Salis-Swabe, who suffered early widowhood after losing her Jewish German husband in 1894, was a founder and benefactor of the Froebel Educational Institute (Weston, 2002). Another is Jane Annie Roadknight, who was an inspirational inspector, promoting Kindergarten practice in the City of Nottingham Education Authority until her retirement in 1919 (Bloomfield, 2000:167–82). Unitarians nowadays may or may not believe in God. They do not believe in the Holy Trinity (Father, Son and Holy Ghost), but they do respect Jesus Christ as a good man. Unitarianism was strong at a point in history (at the turn into the twentieth century) when people were beginning to be influenced by scientific findings and the theories of Charles Darwin and James Wallace rocked traditional Christian religious thinking. There was also, through increased travel opportunities at this period, more exposure to religions other than the Christianity which was dominant in Europe. Other important figures in the early days of the Froebel Educational Institute include Claude Montefiore (Secretary of the Froebel Society 1884–92 and from then on the Chair of the Froebel Educational Institute until his death in 1938) and the principal of the college (1901–31), Esther Lawrence (Principal of the Froebel Educational Institute), both of whom were Jewish. Esther Lawrence gave a speech in the year of the establishment of the League of Nations, which demonstrates the inclusive spirit of the early Froebelians, a part of the legacy of his approach:

> In the children of today lies the hope of the future. Work with and for children is in itself, and notwithstanding it difficulties, full of satisfaction and joy ... let us press forward and realize, through our children, some of the ideals for which the world is striving.
>
> (Lawrence in Weston, 2002:42)

An important question arises. Does it matter that so many Froebelians in the past and today are not Christians, given that this forms a centrepiece of Froebel's educational philosophy? Given that Froebelian education is found across the globe, where educators either embrace a variety of different religions or none, this is an area which needs to be reflected upon and cannot be ignored as the challenge for atheists raised by Jane Whinnett suggests:

> The search for unity is a driving force in Froebel's interpretations of children's actions. Unity is a challenging concept if it is defined in the narrowest sense that Froebel intended it. The child's attempt to create was seen as a metaphor for mankind's attempts to imitate God the creator. For atheists this is a challenging concept. In logical thought, can the whole philosophy be accepted if one vital part of the equation is not proven? Conversely, can practice be totally eclectic and still have meaning? Who constructs the meaning? (2012:62)

A situation exists whereby freethinking educators, who are universalist and of no faith or of faiths other than Christianity, are attracted to, comfortable with and embracing, of the Froebelian philosophy of education as a framework to their work. But it is a fact that Froebel's faith in a Christian God runs deep in his response to life. He remembered throughout his life the texts and quotations from the Bible which he learnt by heart sitting in the vestry of his father's church, listening to his sermons (rather than attending the service itself with what his father saw as distractions). Christianity is central to Froebel's life. It is therefore a straightforward matter to see why educators of deeply committed Christian faith are drawn to his thinking. It is less obvious why educators of a variety of religious faiths and none also find his approach works well for them too. Froebel's concept of *Unity* is the key to this.

An inclusive approach to religion

Christina Dommel (2004) helpfully examines this in depth, suggesting that Froebel was very much of his time but has left an important legacy through his concept of *Unity* which includes, as a deeply important part, his approach to religion. His espousal of an inclusive approach to religious thinking in turn influenced the way he viewed educational institutions such as training colleges, schools and Kindergartens. He was an interesting mix of taking a very individual path in his explorations and yet not rejecting Christianity and was influenced by important thinkers of the day. Dommel points out that,

> Religions today are usually seen as fixed entities with mutually exclusive groups, even in contexts of pluralist or multi-cultural education. This idea would have sounded rather strange to Friedrich Froebel.
>
> (2004:36)

She evidences that Wolfgang von Goethe, who influenced Froebel, was able to read Arabic, and had studied the Qur'an in the original. He was comfortable about being called a Muslim as well as a Christian. Froebel kept a copy of Goethe's writings on the shelf above his desk. Noting that he did not adhere to a fixed view of religion is of great importance when examining the individual way that Froebel's ideas developed and took form through his concept of *Unity*. In many ways, Froebel stayed close to the accepted conventions of the Lutheran Christian Church and remained so throughout his life. But his concept of *Unity* gave him a very individual perspective. The way that there is an interconnectivity in everything pervades his entire educational philosophy:

> The God who plays a crucial role throughout Froebel's work is the panentheistic source of life and growth and transformation, manifested in nature as the principle of unity. He believed that the study of natural history and botany would yield insights of highest moral value. (Dommel, 2004:39)

In Greek, 'panentheism' means *all in God*. God is seen to be in every part of nature yet through being the maker of the universe, is greater. Pantheists simply see God as being in nature and inseparable from it. The description 'panentheism' fits Froebel's beliefs in that he always believed in God as the creator, but perhaps because of his commitment to God being in nature, his thinking did not chime with the teachings of the Lutheran Church of the time. The church authorities were anxious that their congregations might be influenced by the way that the sciences were perceived as opposing religious thinking. It is important to be aware that at this historic point the lack of acceptance of the authority of the Christian church was considered as being irreligious. His schools and Kindergartens came to be banned and were closed in Prussia, following the revolutionary liberalizing ideas that challenged the church and state in 1848. Encouraging children to think for themselves from a young age, supporting and innovating the training of women to be teachers of young Kindergarten age children and embracing, albeit unconsciously, the philosopher Immanuel Kant's thinking on mature moral reasoning were activities that were considered to be dangerous. Froebel's articulations of God are difficult to follow, and he never found a clear way of expressing this. It is through the way in practice that he educated children, young people and adults that his thinking is revealed in action.

The Enlightenment and Romanticism

The major influences on Froebel's thinking, which would, even though not at a conscious or articulated level, have contributed to the development of his concept of *Unity* are the Enlightenment and Romanticism. He does not give any indication that he was aware of these ideas influencing him. He was familiar with the writings of Jacob Boehme, Friedrich von Schiller and Goethe through his father's library, and read their works when he returned to support his father until his death in 1802 in Oberweissbach. Discussion would have been rampant about Rousseau, Pestalozzi, Hegel and Fichte when he studied at Jena from 1794–99 and in the universities of Gottingen (1811–12) and Berlin (1812–13). The interconnectivity across these two main schools of thought, Enlightenment and Romanticism, led him to focus on his individual religious faith and relationship with God through the concept of *Unity* rather than accepting the authority of a church that comes through being part of organized religion.

Resonances with more recent philosophical thinking are also to be found. Michael Foucault's critique of 'regimes of myth' and the importance he places on deciding who you are and want to be and then acting to bring this about (Foucault 1980) connect with Froebel's way of living. In 1967, G. W. Allport wrote a book titled *The Individual and His Religion: A Psychological Interpretation*, suggesting that the language used in relation to organized religion and that of freethinkers often brings the impression of greater difference than what actually exists. Froebel is not unusual in finding it difficult, if not impossible, to put into words his understanding of God. However, Dommel (2004) is clear that Froebel has no desire to deviate from belief in God and the importance of Jesus Christ as a role model and as part of his thoughtful faith. He did not see this as requiring or encouraging children or adult people to try and copy the beliefs guiding his life, 'but with freedom and choice in the way he worked it out in his own individual circumstances' (Smith, 1983:309).

Paradoxes – inclusive – conventional – individual commitment to a Christian God

Eglantyne Mary Jebb (1953:11) who was principal of the Froebel Educational Institute in Roehampton from 1931 to 1955 felt that Froebel came to very individual religious views which were 'essentially his own' as a result of personal and very intense personal experiences. She wrote:

> He threw hell overboard as he threw original sin but kept heaven. A Christian spirit but not a Christian dogma marks his religious attitude. (Jebb, 1953:11)

In other words, the individual holding of thoughtful faith is different from conforming to and belonging to an organized religion exerting authority over the individual. Froebel's religious, personal faith and relationship with God was not conventional. In interesting ways Froebel managed both an individual religious belief and a closeness to the traditional Lutheran Church. This was easier to achieve during his period in history and cultural context than it would be now, when fixed forms of religious beliefs prevail. Froebel's embracing of both his own thinking about God and his close adherence to church traditions, for example, through traditional readings of the Bible, makes it easier for those of one or the other persuasions to engage with his educational approach and to join in the search and exploration of the concept of *Unity*. Becoming self-aware, seeing how, through self-knowledge, communities and individuals can come together in positive ways and make a better world, and engaging with issues of the universe as part of that, are at the heart of the concept of *Unity*.

Marion Smith, a lecturer in the Religious Education Department at the Froebel Educational Institute in the late 1960s notes that,

> At that time many people wanted to find some unifying principle in the whole. Certain scientific studies both influenced them, and perhaps made it seem as though the search would succeed. (Smith, 1983:306)

This may account for Froebel's restless searching for the laws of nature through forestry, botany, mathematics and crystallography. This science precedes Darwin but the emergent journey towards his theory of evolution is there, explored by liberal thinkers like Goethe. Froebel was also interested in Jacob Boehme's concept of 'becoming', which suggested that both people and the world itself are in a process of becoming (Smith, 1983:307).

The illustration in Figure 2.1 demonstrates some of the central messages of Froebel's concept of *Unity* with three guiding themes. First, he introduces

FIGURE 2.1 The little gardener, from the *Mutter und Koselieder*.

interactive physical play with the *Finger Play* of the song, highlighting the importance of nurturing relationships. Second, the garden opens up a world of knowledge for the child. The elderly man in the background is offered produce from the garden that the child has chosen and been helped to grow. There is symbolic meaning. The child, without external pressure, wants to participate in making the world a better place. There is a relationship between the *inner* and the *outer*. An understanding of what causes what and how different things connect is developing. Caring for plants in the garden links with caring for people who need food.

Inclusive schools

During Froebel's life, contexts of organized religion in the separate German states were present in both the churches and educational institutions. Churches, schools and colleges followed the religion of the local duke. Froebel's schools and Kindergartens pioneered secular, universalist educa-tion and this has been a tradition which has to a great extent been sustained in other parts of the world. Although his religious thinking was central to his own life, Froebel was not driven by a need to focus on religious dif-ferences between people or religious institutions. The term 'secularism' did not come into being until after his death in 1852 (Dommel (2004:38–9). Froebel developed the Helba Plan, which was never implemented, in which he hoped, supported with funding by the Duke of Meiningen, to educate Jewish and Christian children together leaving them to choose at 14 years of age whether they would like to receive Jewish or Christian religious edu-cation. He worked with close friends and colleagues who were liberal Jews. This gives a good demonstration of the closeness Froebel felt towards the conventional educational practice of Christian teaching in schools of the day, alongside his very individual approach which is more secular in spirit. There is no dichotomy here. Instead there is an interesting entanglement. Things are more subtle than might at first be apparent. It might look as if Froebel is inconsistent and muddled. In fact, he is of his time in many respects in relation to religious teaching.

It took many years for his individual approach to develop more clarity, and this emerged in the foundation of the Kindergarten in 1837. Secular, inclusive education was introduced and pioneered in the Kindergarten move-ment that he invented. For those who maintain that faith schools are crucial in avoiding the exclusion and possible extinction of religion in any society or culture, secular education is a challenge. But for those who believe that when children, whose families hold different faiths or none, come together and are encouraged to think about the universe, from climate change to farming, how peaceful living is achieved and to become self-aware through the concept of Froebelian *Unity*, secular inclusive education is a positive way forward for humanity. It provides a safe place for everyone. Dommel writes, that 'we need to maintain the institutional secular space in order to guarantee religious freedom and plurality' (2004:45).

The goodness of children

Froebel had great confidence in the fundamental goodness of children, and it was part of his concept of *Unity* to believe that this was because God was in them. For this reason, he did not give them Bible texts to learn or religious songs to sing. He believed that children move from literal to abstract thinking, and this kind of literature was, in his view too abstract for them to make meaning such that they could act on what was given to them. He thought that children should not be burdened with

> a great deal of oppressive load of extraneous and merely external information and culture. (Froebel, 1899:231)

He did not teach subjects separately or provide religious education in a formal sense. Instead, he wanted to help children make connections between things and people. If a child could make maximum use of their everyday lives, see the beauty in the patterns of things and come to see the meanings held in the arts, sciences and humanities, this would bring them nearer to the *Unity* that is in all things. By becoming self-aware, being connected to other people and understanding them, being sympathetic and seeing how and when they need help and support and teamwork, and connecting their everyday lives with increasingly abstract thoughts, they would find fulfilment. It is important to bear in mind that Froebel did not have as his aim the happiness of children and humanity. His thinking chimes with Kant's moral reasoning and the importance of helping children into a way of becoming that equips them to think things out:

> So, gradually, each person would become able to act and respond to the unexpected or testing situation, in a way which he would not afterwards regret because he had acted in accord with what he truly thought. (Froebel in Lilley, 1967:95)

The problem of emphasis on extrinsic motivation

Froebel had noticed that after the death of his father – who was stern, and punished wrongdoing and rebuked his parishioners endlessly – people quickly became undisciplined once the control of his authority was removed. This was not so in his maternal uncle's parish. After his uncle's death, having experienced kindness, understanding and supportive discussions, people continued to act according to the values espoused by his uncle. He valued the fulfilment that comes from striving to make a better world rather than the pursuit of happiness. Fulfilment is more likely to bring happiness of a deeper kind than the fluctuating and temporary state that comes with trying to satisfy only the self, without doing so within the contexts of others and the world they inhabit.

This might sound over idealistic, but Froebel spent enough time with children to try out his 'infallible remedy' and because of his own childhood struggles to be good, he was on the child's side where naughtiness and disobedience featured. He accepted that children are at times both disobedient and naughty. But how the adult responds to this is key:

> Under each human fault lies a good tendency which has been crushed, misunderstood or misled. Hence the infallible remedy for all wickedness is first to bring to light this original good tendency and then to nourish, foster and train it. (Froebel, 1897:121)

In Chapter Seven the importance of observation is explored. Froebel writes about the problem of teachers who do not engage in observation. They are not then able to tune into children and so they are insensitive towards them. Froebel felt that,

> Unhappily there are among teachers those unfortunate persons who always see children as mischievous, spiteful, cunning little devils, whereas others see at most an over exuberant sense of life or a situation which has got out of hand. (Froebel in Lilley, 1967:135)

In order to help children to act in ways which chime with his concept of *Unity*, children and adults need to learn through each other (Liebschner, [1992]2001; 1985). Hence what has become the famous Froebelian dictum:

> Let us impart life to ourselves; to our children; Let us live through them, give meaning to our speech and life and the things about us. Let us live with them and let them live with us; thus shall we obtain through them what we all need. (Froebel, 1897:88)

Part of this quotation is carved in stonework above the building entrance of the Helsinki Kindergarten teacher training college, now a museum. Froebel is aware that adults often reprimand children by shouting at them and hitting them. He points out that,

> Children are often punished by adults for faults which they have in fact learnt from them. (Froebel in Lilley, 1967:136)

His careful observations of the behaviour of children show how children appreciate being treated with respect with their efforts valued, and how this brings out the best in them. He notes the way they will offer gifts, such as drawings as a way of expressing their appreciation. As Froebel says:

> The good-natured child values only that which can serve as a shared possession, a bond of union between himself and those he loves. This should be noticed by parents and teachers and used to arouse and develop his impulse to activity and expression. No gifts, however small, which a child makes, should ever be disregarded. (Froebel in Lilley, 1967:38)

In Chapter Eight the value Froebel placed on becoming part of and contributing to a community of learners is illuminated. It helps the process of self-awareness as well as bringing sensitivity and a tuning into the needs of others. To have this as a foundation to later participation and striving to create a better world is a strong reason why Froebel came to value the Kindergarten and the education it offered children. Jane Whinnett reflects on the learning, across a year, of 4-year-old Ross:

> I experienced the wholeness of his learning both in each part of the planning and reflecting on the documentation when he moved on to school. For me the unity comes from conceptual coherence in the experiences offered, the level of involvement in those experiences and the relevance of the experiences to the child's intentions. (2006:76)

She goes on to quote from Froebel's letter:

> I am firmly convinced that all the phenomena of the child-world, those which delight us as well as grieve us, depend upon fixed laws as definite as those of the cosmos, the planetary system, and the operations of nature: and it is therefore impossible to discover them and examine them. (Froebel's Letter VIII, Murray, 1929:14)

Froebel is always striving for the law of *Unity*.

Enlightenment, Romanticism or postmodernism? Does Froebel's approach to life chime with any of these philosophically?

Spending time alone in early and middle childhood led Froebel to become reflective and analytical about his experiences. This may be why he is so often placed in the Romantic category. Evelyn Lawrence (1952:3) was director of the National Froebel Foundation and makes reference to a letter Froebel wrote in 1827. She suggests that his father influenced what she terms 'the transcendental philosophy' he developed. Probably by this she means that his ideas were influenced by the idealism of the European Romantic movement. The philosopher Stephen Law sees Romanticism as embracing 'the unity of nature, with each particle of matter and each mind being a microcosm reflecting the whole, stressing the fundamental continuity between self, world and the divine' (2007:307). This does seem to chime with Froebel's writings on *Unity*. It is also the case that the influence on Froebel of the Romantic ideas in Goethe's writings are evident. Froebel certainly challenged tradition, dogma and authority and believed in the autonomous thinking and freedom of the individual.

However, nothing is straightforward, and much of Froebel's philosophy of life also seems to chime with German Enlightenment thinking, which came earlier than the Romanticism that developed during the nineteenth century. He was trained in mathematics and what was then the cutting-edge science of crystallography and emergent chemistry, which in important ways linked to the rational principles of German Enlightenment thinking (also known as the age of reason in France) and led to scientific and social progress.

Froebel does not quite fit into either the Romantic or the Enlightenment categories. Although he was associated with the scientific revolution that was occurring, he did not see as a new god the science which many free thinkers adopted. His view of God was not the conventional Lutheran form, but God remained central in his life and in his approach to education. In this sense, he is more inclined to a transcendental or Romantic philosophy of life. This means that he cannot be placed in a philosophical or religious box. His way of working throughout his life intuitively draws on both the legacy of the Enlightenment of the eighteenth century and the emergence of the Romanticism of transcendental thought in the nineteenth century. The latter promoted an emotional response to life experiences, spontaneity and creativity, individualism and being in tune with nature. However, he was probably more an Enlightenment thinker than a Romantic. This is because he valued the contribution to and participation in the community and working towards the betterment of the world in all its aspects. This element of his approach was a major part of the Keilhau school which he founded, and this vein of thinking was continued and implemented in the Kindergarten approach he invented in Blankenburg.

The relationship between the child as an individual and the child as a participating member of a community was something which occupied Froebel's energy in forming his approach to education. His law of *Unity* was central to this. Froebel was not a conformist himself, and he did not expect the children in his school to bow in unthinking ways to the external authority of the teacher. But on the other hand, he went about educating children to want to be contributors to their community, and as they matured, to contribute on a wider scale. Is there a conflict here? Is there a tension between wanting children to have the freedom to be themselves and also wanting to guide children to learn responsibility and to contribute to the world? *Freedom with guidance* is after all one of the cornerstones of Froebelian education. It is not possible to place Froebel's approach easily. This is because his concept of *Unity* requires freedom for the individual but, because it locates self-awareness in relationship with others and the wider world, the *Unity* he strives to create also involves guidance. This means that he is neither an individualistic Romantic nor a wholly rationalist thinker of the Enlightenment.

Postmodernism is relevant here because it has critiqued the established views of discipline and power. Foucault (1980) advocates for people to become individuals, who are capable of shaping their own subjectivity. This involves examining things in order to see how they are and consciously deciding how to act, or to put it another way, deciding who to be. G. Dahlberg, P. Moss and A. Pence ([1999]2013:34) suggest that Foucault's approach places *thought* at the centre. Through encouraging thinking, children from an early age are able to ponder and get to grips with established ideas and to develop new thoughts. This, in Foucault's view, gives freedom because it helps children to be detached from expectations to act and do things in particular ways. There is a resonance here which gives exactly the kind of freedom that the Froebelian Kindergarten or school for older children pioneered. It may even have contributed to the Verbot edict to close Froebel's Kindergarten schools in Saxony in 1851. But, although children were encouraged to reflect and tease things out and to act in accordance with their thoughts, Froebel, unlike Foucault, placed great value on *freedom with guidance*.

Dahlberg, Moss and Pence ([1999]2013:33) refer to J. Ransom (1997:143) who points out that there is some connection between what Foucault says and what Kant says. Kant argues that we need to use our capacity to reason so that we can bring order to both our own lives and to the world we inhabit. This is to do with the question of maturity. It is helpful in getting to grips with the Froebelian position. Froebel's values sit most easily beside the work of the giant of philosophy, Immanuel Kant (1724–1804). He examined the constraining impact of both political and religious authority. Kant was fascinated by the relationship between the freedom to be an individual and how this links to authority in the political sense. He investigated the role of ethics in this regard. The power of reason is brought to bear in making moral decisions. The decision may not benefit the person making the decision, and so it is about the duty to fulfil what is a universal need. If people act out of compassion, or through feeling a sense of guilt or to serve their own self-interest, this is not a moral behaviour. It is only moral when the fulfilment of duty comes, and this is brought about through our ability to reason as an autonomous person.

Time and again Froebel's position returns us to the moral issues, and to the place of moral authority. There is a connection here with Foucault's approach to authority, in that children are supported in developing their own thinking in relation to who they want to be. Perhaps Froebel's own childhood experiences have been a major influence in this. He had to deal with stern external authority from both his father and his stepmother in his early and middle childhood. The contrast with the way authority was applied when he moved to be with his uncle's gentler family context must have been thought-provoking, and would have shaped his approach as to how best to encourage children to respond to school authority and the rules laid down. But Froebel is more linked to Kant than Foucault in his concern for how a sense of duty and the self-discipline that goes with that, comes about. How children are supported so that they autonomously begin to develop a sense of commitment to making a better world as a reason for living was a matter of great importance for him. Froebel linked *freedom* with *guidance* in his educational approach seeing this as part of the *Unity* of relationship between self-awareness, others and the world as a whole universe. Self-awareness is connected both to other people and the material, physical world. Again here, his own life experiences shape the view he comes to hold. He was a Lutheran Christian, but not a conventional one. He could be described as Foucauldian in the way he shaped his own thinking within the Christian church and yet in important ways, through a developing self-awareness, concurrently moved out of that box. It is perhaps the sense of moral duty that self-awareness brings in the Froebelian approach which takes a different slant from Foucault. However, Froebel, Kant and Foucault meet on the matter of maturity. Enabling mature thinking is what the three of them aim for. This requires autonomy of thought, which means knowing what you think, knowing what you need help with and knowing how to find appropriate help that is needed without losing your *self* in the process.

Unity: How everything links from whole to parts (not parts to whole)

Froebel's concept of *Unity* is central to his holistic way of thinking. Within this emphasis on the wholeness of life he also locates interconnectivity as being of fundamental importance. Everything links and is interdependent. 'Link, always link' is a central tenet of Froebelianism. It is not a question of separate parts being identified and then learning how they come together to make the whole. It is the reverse. The whole enables the possibility to see, understand and use the parts, their function and purpose. This is consistent throughout the Froebelian framework. Froebel's concept of *Unity* is concerned with the developing self-awareness that emerges through sustained connection with and linking to learning through and with others and relationship with matters of the universe. In this way, Froebelian education leads children and adults involved in it to live in a world concerned with what is of universal importance. This occurs while at the same time finding through knowledge of the self, ways of contributing to the community and perhaps beyond. A sense of fulfilment results. The interconnectivity between, self -awareness, relationship with others and the universe are key to the concept of *Unity*.

The concept of *Unity* infuses the way in which children are educated. For example, it guides teachers in the way that children are taught with enjoyment to write, read, understand mathematics and the place of numeracy within that. In this respect Froebelians have been challenged by the phonics first and fast model adopted by the English government as well as the emphasis on number rather than mathematics. Froebelians go to the source of literacy as a beginning, with a focus on communication and language or signing, extended through stories with and without books, through *Finger Plays* and action games with songs and rhymes. They encourage a fusion of making meaning, from the texts children are introduced to, supporting their typically spontaneous early attempts at writing, building an understanding of the relationships between sentences, words and letters with sounds (Bruce and Spratt, 2011). In Froebelian educational settings, children are not early readers in the main, though some are. Children become good readers and writers by the time they reach middle childhood, supported by a wealth of experiences which they bring to communicating, language and literacy. Perhaps the most important thing is that, more often than not, they continue to be bookworms and enthusiastic readers and writers, engaging with both literature, non-fiction and they do so for the rest of their lives. When life is experienced in interconnected ways, education is thorough, sound and enthusiastically embraced.

Mathematical learning is also linked to what Froebel came to term the *Forms of everyday life, beauty and knowledge* of mathematics itself. This inevitably links the mathematics to other areas of knowledge in the arts and humanities. An example is given in the booklet by Finnish Froebelians working at the Ebeneser Foundation/Kindergarten Museum in Helsinki (2019) in which Reeta Niemela, Alexander Reichstein and Taina Sillanpaa guide adults into providing ways of supporting and extending children in making meaning of spheres, cubes, cylinders, prisms and other shapes in the world, as in the table at a mealtime, or in the garden.

The concept of *Unity* influences how children are taught the humanities including geography and history, such as finding the source of a river, by following it back to a stream, or finding clay in a London garden, or chalk on a cliff. Seeing which trees grow in the park, near the bus stop and watching the rooks gathering on a building in the early evening or knowing where the sun sets, and what the clouds mean in relation to the weather. It involves a very hands-on and practical approach to learning about the sciences, so that children understand in meaningful ways how science connects to their everyday life and the world beyond. These examples demonstrate this – there is evaporation when drying your clothes after washing them, gravity when a toddler (accidentally?) splashes custard or a biscuit crumbles and drops to the ground, waiting for your porridge to cool or melting chocolate to make a sauce. Linking things together into whole aspects of science through everyday life is of particular educational use at a time of climate change, global warming and digital advance. Froebel's embracing of the arts, dance, music, drama, literature, poetry and visual arts (both three-dimensional and two-dimensional), also emphasizes interconnectivity with both science and the humanities. For example, using local clay makes links to cultural contexts of pottery and representational activities and to the sources of clay in the earth and its human, plant and animal use across time and space.

A Froebelian teacher

The Froebelian concept of *Unity* is a complex matter. In 1999, I was invited by Professor Lesley Abbott (the Froebelian who led the *Birth to Three Matters* Framework for the government DfES in the English context 2002) to write a chapter in a book for the millennium. I wrote about 'Teachers who inspired me':

> The appreciation young children feel for the rest of their lives towards those adults who have contributed in a major way to how they feel about themselves as learners is rarely spoken. It is an abstract, intuitive thing which they take with them through their lives. And yet, it anchors them forever, and it is sometimes called having a sense of well-being … [G]ood teachers help you to learn the things you find hardest in ways which are right for you. (Bruce, 2020:24 and 26)

In this quotation from the book, it is possible to see the Froebelian approach. The *symbolic life* is strongly present. The adult demonstrates how to use one thing to represent another. There is the desk that become a radio. She encourages drawing as interconnected with writing. There is music, with folk songs and nursery songs (not the Mother songs or action songs though). The playground of the school is small and the ground is covered with tarmac, so she grows beans in the classroom to give children some *Engagement with Nature*. Mathematics is linked to the *Forms of everyday life* through the shopping. The presentation of the shop and work cards as part of it gave *Beauty* and mathematical *Knowledge* had a central place. Her teaching caused thought (something Froebel believed to be a central part of education) as children used parquetry and made stick patterns. These were *Occupations,* as was the clay. The *symbolic life* was given a high priority through the storytelling, reading of stories and the acting out and dancing. The Froebelian concept of *Unity* beams out of the teaching of the Froebelian, Joyce Greaves:

> At seven years of age, I moved to the top infants class to be with the Froebel trained Joyce Greaves. We did radio plays, pretending to switch her desk off and on like a wireless. We decorated our handwriting books. She read us poetry and played songs on the piano. We used clay, did collage, made models, grew beans in jam jars, had a shop with lovely work cards for our maths, made patterns with wooden shapes (I now know these were Froebel's Occupations), found places on the globe and looked at artefacts found in different countries and cultures. We did stories in dance, song and drama, and got in rather a mess when making animals out of clay. (Bruce, 2020:25)

CHAPTER THREE

Engagement with Nature

Engagement with Nature is key to being a Froebelian. This has become an even greater priority since the recognition that the issue of climate change has become an urgent matter to address. Looking at what it means to 'engage' through recent studies of the brain indicate that, for example, listening to music is not the same as learning to play an instrument or singing in a choir (Ross, Barat and Fujioka, 2017). In the same way, sitting in the garden listening to birdsong and enjoying the experience, going for walks in the countryside or sitting on the beach are not necessarily ways of engaging with nature. They are ways of enjoying nature.

Engaging with nature is an active learning process. It links with the development of awareness of self in relationship with nature and people. How we, for example, use plastic or avoid it, grow and eat our food, packaged or not, travel and explore on this planet and in outer space impacts on other people, animal welfare, the sea, the growing of plants, the universe. We can do what we can as individuals by shopping carefully, gardening or avoiding fossil fuel. But it requires a global group effort which takes a long-term view rather than the short-termism typical of governments in different countries of the world to deal with climate change. This chapter argues that children are helped into thinking about and acting on these universal and huge challenges to life on earth by engaging with nature through the activities in their everyday lives. Making connections between trees and wooden furniture or their playthings and if they are made of plastic, viewing short film extracts showing the importance of creatures in the sea and what is important for the survival of sea life and its habitats make the learning experiences easy to comprehend. Gardening and then eating the tomatoes or picking the apples from the ground under the trees gives another engagement. Seeing how bees visit the flowers and learning why spiders and ants are important through seeing them in action in the garden takes any fear away from mini-beasts and turns into appreciation of their importance.

Froebelian symbolic imagery connected with nature: the lily

Jacob Boehme, the seventeenth-century Silesian mystic, influenced Froebel's relationship with nature. He would have been introduced to his writings through his father's German Protestantism (Lilley, 1967:17). This led to his use of imagery connected to nature. The lily, garden and the linden tree were powerful metaphors for him. There is still a linden tree outside the school in Keilhau. It is impossible to know if there is any significance in the fact that the ceiling in the sitting room of the house in which Froebel was born has a lily design. When the Froebel Trust was founded in 2010, the lily on the logo formed a brand image which showed a powerful historic continuation of tradition from the founding logo and brand image of the Froebel Educational Institute in 1894 to the Froebel Trust. There is pressure from current Froebelians to sustain the imagery and metaphor dating back to Froebelian origins.

The lily brooch, the inspired idea of Jane Whinnett, became a logo and brand image for the founders of the Edinburgh Froebel Network (2008) (Figure 3.1). Other Froebelian networks have adopted their own versions, using a variety of lily designs. The lily logo has been taken by the Travelling Froebel Tutor Group who teach the Froebel Trust Short Courses. The tutors for the Elinor Goldschmied Froebel Group, South African and Kolkata Froebelian groups and Froebel network in Australia have all adopted the lily. These lily logos can be regarded as a Romantic and sentimental response on the part of tutors working within the Froebelian framework of education. Or the lilies can be seen as the result of searching for an appropriate logo and brand image that is fit for purpose today and encapsulates the Froebelian philosophy and metaphor in a simple visual way. The metaphor of the lily included in a Froebelian logo as a brand image brings a sense of belonging, continuity, a connection with Froebel's philosophical influences, with nature, the universe, *Unity,* the *symbolic life,* and the *Forms.* The lily in Europe grows in dark, dank places, where there is no expectation of anything beautiful growing. In South Africa, the red fire lily is the first flower to emerge after the fynbos fires. In India, the lily on the logo is the only flower that can cling to the highest mountains. In the Australian outback this lily survives the intense heat. For Froebelians taking forward the work of the Froebelian Elinor Goldschmied with babies the willow Treasure Basket she designed is widely used. The loving adult offers nurture, intellectual possibilities and protection, just as the communal garden surrounds the gardens of the children. The Falkirk Froebel Network lily (Figure 3.2) emerged as a study aid for the regular meetings of the group. One visual image is worth a thousand words.

The way in which Froebel saw connectedness in nature and in children's development is relevant here. Because a child is growing up in challenging

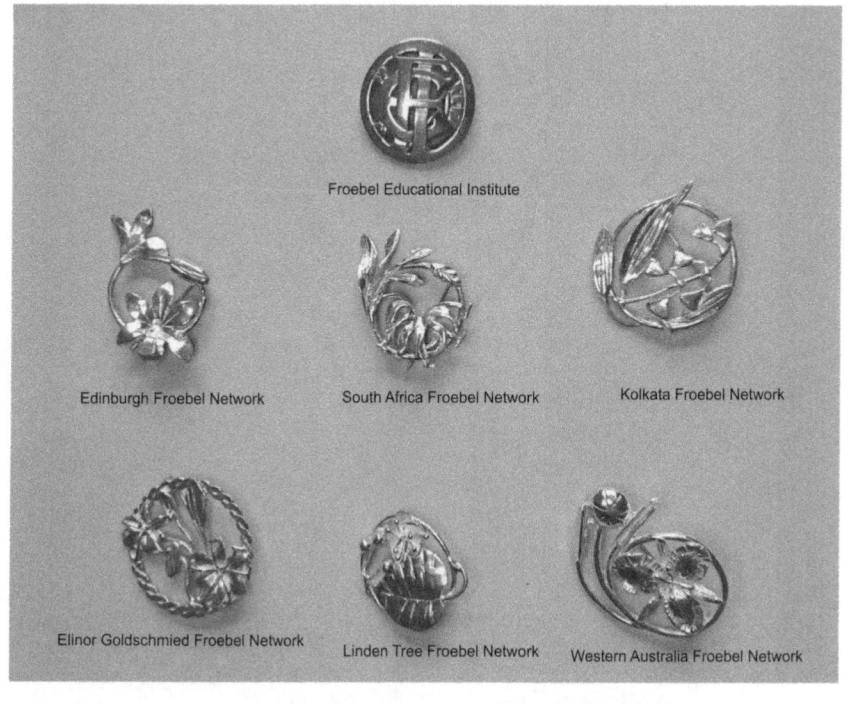

Froebel Educational Institute

Edinburgh Froebel Network

South Africa Froebel Network

Kolkata Froebel Network

Elinor Goldschmied Froebel Network

Linden Tree Froebel Network

Western Australia Froebel Network

FIGURE 3.1 The Froebel lilies and linden tree (brooches designed by Sheana M. Stephen DA).

circumstances, it does not mean that there is no hope that they can become well educated and flourish in life, provided that they are looked for, identified and their strengths are nutured.

Susan Herrington expands on the symbolic aspects of the Froebelian garden:

> The notion of using the garden both as a source of food and a prophetic image of the integration of man and nature is relevant to the most fundamental definitions of a garden. By using the garden to describe his school and by designing gardens as the physical counterpart to his educational philosophy, Froebel participated in a long-standing tradition of garden design.
>
> (1998:326)

Just as plants such as the lily are symbolic, so Froebel gave the metaphor of plants being symbolic of the child's own development. For Froebel both the garden and the landscape beyond, where there are wilder places, are important. He felt that the garden is 'an idealised culture secure from the outside world' (Herrington, 1998:334). Herrington suggests that the Kindergarten

FIGURE 3.2 The Falkirk Froebel Network logo.

garden portrays in a coded form the *interconnectedness* and *Unity* that is central to Froebel's educational approach. She argues that there is a yearning to reconnect with German folk art and a society that is at ease with nature in Froebel's idea of a garden, which is in contrast with the understanding of the Prussian government and monarchy of Frederick William IV who felt that such images of peasant and folk culture are dangerously supportive of German nationalism and revolution. She gives examples from the *Mother Play and Nursery Songs* (1844) and *Mother Songs, Games and Stories* (1895) which give these images in both the illustrations and the words of the songs:

> The notion of the garden as a representational image of the relationship between man and nature or an idealised society is a primary reason why cultures create gardens. Understanding Froebel's kindergarten as part of this tradition gives logic to Froebel's use of the garden as a conscious art form and an educational tool, both metaphorically and experientially. (Herrington, 1998:337)

Why outdoor learning is important

Helen Tovey is a leading expert in the Froebelian approach to the outdoor environment. She is a Froebel Trust tutor for the courses in Scotland and the Travelling Tutor courses throughout the UK. She writes about being a Froebelian in the world of today:

> The garden is the essence of a Froebelian early years setting. It offers space to move freely and expansively. To run, leap and frolic, and to play with abandon. It is a dynamic environment which is always full of surprise, and a place for moving, thinking, feeling, imagining and creating. ... Direct experience of nature was essential to Froebel. Children learnt *in* nature rather than just *about* nature. Through gardening and play outdoors children were immersed in the natural world and could learn about the growth of plants and animals, about the beauty of nature and about the inter-relationships of all living things. (Tovey, 2017:64–5, emphasis in the original)

The strands that Tovey identifies are evident in the school in Keilhau, in the first Kindergarten in Blankenburg and in the subsequent Kindergartens that Froebel founded. There are opportunities for children to move with freedom in the outdoor garden, and there are endless possibilities to learn in and about nature itself beyond the garden. Helen Tovey writes about the organization of the outdoor garden and outings. She is acutely aware that many children today are growing up in urban contexts. She points out the importance of children experiencing 'rough ground, uneven surfaces and wild areas'. She emphasizes the contribution to physical development that these experiences make. She also reminds Froebelians of the way outdoor play nurtures and cultivates the imagination and collaboration between children as well as the practitioners and intergenerational members of their families. The aspect of gardening for vegetables, fruits and flowers is also present. As she says:

> A Froebelian environment provides resources which can be transformed rather than bought equipment which is 'pre-formed'. It is the act of trans-formation which is important as it involves children in symbolic thinking, using one object to stand for another. (Tovey, n.d.: n.p.)

Play matters. It is part of the sensory experiences that children have. The *symbolic life* is empowered in the garden. Imagining that plants are people is an example. I remember playing schools in the garden and teaching a group of snapdragons. When it was lunchtime in the school, I fed them by opening their petals and dropping in water. With my brother Marc, I made bird's nests with the grass cuttings after the grass was mown. I sailed ships with him, climbing trees to make the rigging. We hid from 'baddies' behind bushes. We administered the injured with dock leaves to relieve stings. We made church services chanting in processions and burning lavender in old tea infusers to make incense. We rescued princesses from ogres. We used dressing up clothes and we made props.

Froebel's plan for the Kindergarten garden

Early diagrams of the Kindergarten garden design emerge in Froebel's publi-cation of his 'Journal of education' (April 1850). He drew up plans using his previously acquired skills as a surveyor and land manager (Figure 3.3). As is always the case with Froebel, he did not make standardized plans. Each garden in each Kindergarten was unique to the landscape and cultural con-text. But there are common elements present in each. In other words, there is difference in the sameness.

Around the outer boundary is a communal garden which surrounds the individual gardens of the children. When there are constraints in space, children share gardens but, ideally, they are 4 feet square. There are nar-row paths between the children's gardens. The main paths connecting to the communal gardens are wide enough for two children to walk side by side. The first names of the children are marked on sticks and placed in their garden. The children choose what they would like to grow:

In their own little beds the children can plant what and how they will, also ideal with the plants as they will, that they must learn from their own injurious treatment that plants also cannot grow well unless they are treated carefully according to laws. This will be shown to them by plants in the common bed, which they must observe carefully, so that they may calmly notice them in their development from seed through germination, growing, blossoming and fructifying to the seed again. (Froebel, 1912:221)

The natural landscapes beyond the garden

Actively gardening is an example of Froebel's concept of *freedom with guidance* and completion as part of the concept of *Unity*. Beyond the garden there is a wilder nature landscape. In the *Education of Man* Froebel sets out a description of the scenery surrounding Keilhau and wishes the children to explore the stream to its source, to climb and survey the valley from a height and so on with adults. This would be a great challenge in an urban context such as Whitechapel in the inner city and densely populated London. But a short bus ride to the 23acre deconsecrated cemetery at Mile End provides a rich experience of nature. It also provides possibilities to connect with the cultural context. Direct first-hand experiences go far beyond an explanation in words. Having such experiences also creates possibilities for genuine conversations, some 'in the moment' and some later in ways which are authentic, rather than question and answer sessions imposed by adults. According to Froebel,

Where this sense of Nature is still unspoilt, nothing unites teacher and pupil so closely as a common effort to study its phenomena. Teachers should regularly take their classes out of doors – not driving them out like a flock of sheep or leading them as if they were a company of soldiers, but walking with them as a father or sons or a brother with his brothers and making them more familiar with whatever Nature or the season offers. (Froebel, in Lilley, 1967:146)

Jane Read writes about Mrs Shaw, who despite being refused permission by the Education Department in 1895 to take her class in Hackney to Epping Forest, took sixty children during the weekend:

This was the first of a regular series of outings lasting throughout her time at Church Street. They collected nature study specimens for lessons but also stocking the aquarium with snails, caddisflies, worms, and so on from the ponds. They also sent the children's work to the Nature Study Exhibition at the botanical gardens at Kew. This was a wonderful

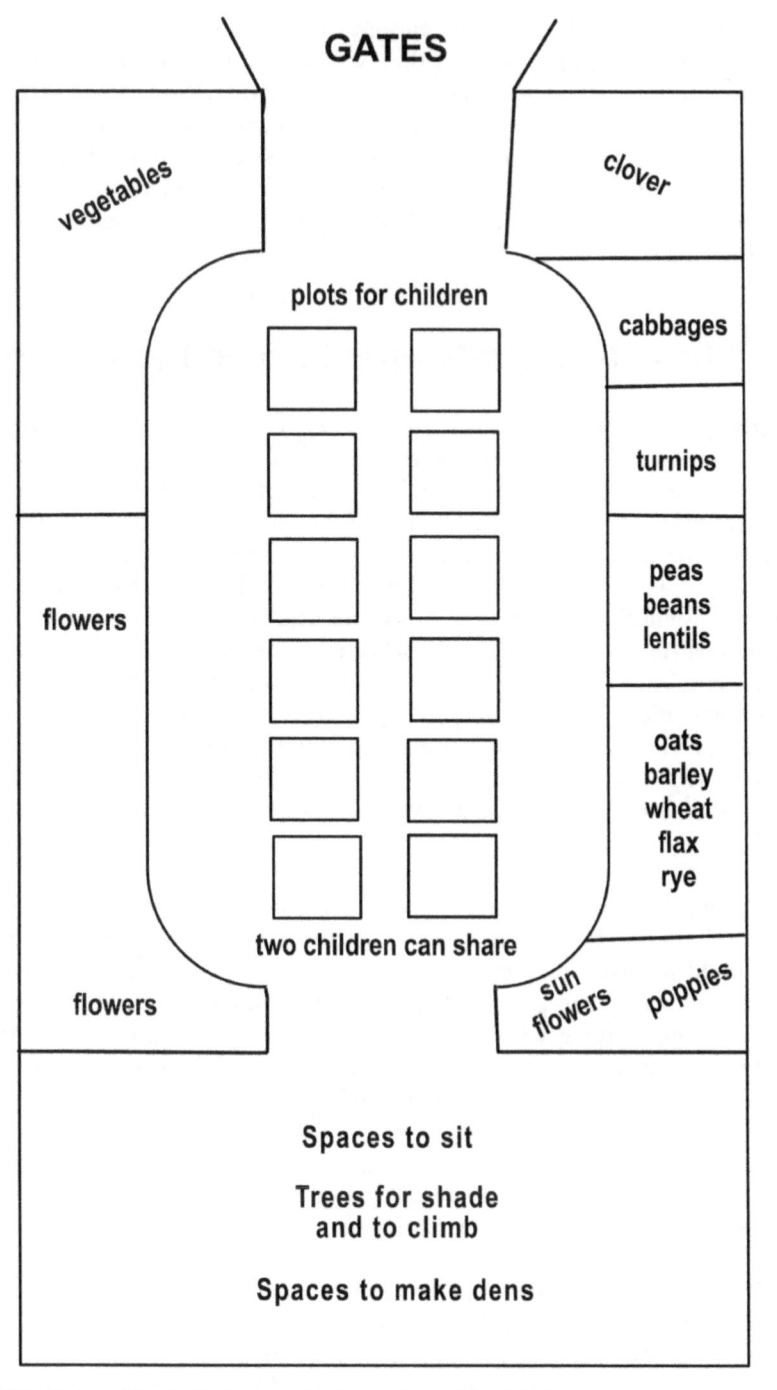

FIGURE 3.3 Froebel's design for the garden of the Kindergarten.

experience for these children; others had similar experiences in the voluntary settings which opened from 1900, the free kindergartens. (Read, 2012:75)

Froebel's vision of nature was enmeshed with the culture of his time and the philosophy that surrounded him. Children would, he hoped, become gardeners, but they would also grow as human beings in the protected space created for them within the community in the garden. They would explore, discover and engage with nature, both directly and symbolically in the garden. Although he never studied philosophy Kant, Goethe Boehme all influenced him. The garden and the landscape beyond form a nuanced and layered experience. It is how the world can be ideally, but there needs to be stewardship of the planet and community by the people who inhabit it. The children and community are not cut off from the world of nature. This is not an isolated safe haven. The garden and the landscape beyond are places that consistently cause thought. This is because they are engaged with in ways that results in actions towards making a better world. The children and trained Kindergarten teachers who have experienced such times immersed in nature certainly seem to act on the thinking that comes through their Froebelian education. Examples are threaded throughout this book.

Rural situations and urban life

It is interesting that Froebel chose to develop his educational framework in a rural context. This was a combination of the need to be able to experiment in developing the educational approach at some distance away from official pressures and scrutiny, the financial necessity of the lower expenditure in a rural setting, and his deep appreciation, knowledge and *Engagement with Nature* as something central in his life. What is also interesting is that those Froebelians who followed immediately after him often worked in urban contexts. For example, the first Kindergarten in England was that of Bertha Ronge (1851). The Kindergarten was in a house in Hampstead in London, and she began training Kindergarten teachers and was active in the Froebel Society (Read, 2019a:15). But these early Kindergartens tended to be located in the homes of middle-class Froebelians. Gardens were often small, at the back of town houses, although the children still had some access to outdoor learning both as part of their attendance at the Kindergarten and at home. Jane Read (2012:72–3) highlights Froebel's recognition of the way parents can be encouraged to value outdoor learning. She points out the way in which he suggested that children might help with household tasks in the garden, such as chopping, sawing and piling wood. Children will ask: Why? What is it for? They will learn the purpose of these activities. They will like to play in sand and clay and with water, damming pools, making rivulets, learning their scientific properties as they do so. They will also learn about growing plants, and parents can help them learn about the importance of bees, beetles, birds, butterflies and the creation of animal habitats.

Jane Read writes a fascinating account of the way in which the street play of children from poorer families became viewed in urban contexts during the late nineteenth and early twentieth centuries:

> The gutter play of working class children was characterised as dirty; the street was an inappropriate and unregulated space for young children, where experiences were socially damaging, to themselves and to society at large and of dubious educational value. (Read, 2019b:268)

This contrasts starkly with the way the play of middle-class children in a rural garden, supervised by adults, was typically valued highly. Read illuminates key issues of Froebelian outdoor learning quoting Margaret McMillan (1930:47) invented the nursery school and was a trained and active Froebelian, working in an area of great poverty. She wrote of the school in Deptford:

> Our green plots and ordered walks are good and right, but who does not remember that he once liked to play in a big place, where there are no walks at all, and no rules. Therefore, a Nursery garden must have a free and rich place, a great rubbish heap, stones, flints, bits of can, and old iron and pots. (Read, 2019b:268)

The fight to keep gardens, even regulated ones, as part of the outdoor classroom environment in education continues. So often there is now a small paved and safety surfaced area with unimaginative climbing frames and a few wheeled vehicles and perhaps a small sandpit. In England the government, supported by the English inspection organization Office for Standards in Education (Ofsted) began to allow settings, particularly in the private sector, to operate in environments with little or no outdoor provision. The only stipulation was for children to be taken out each day to a park for a short time. The opportunity to ensure high quality outdoor learning in every setting was missed, with the documents that became legally framed and implemented 'Curriculum Guidance for the Foundation Stage' in 2000 and 'Birth to Three Matters' in 2002. The efforts to create gardens that are Froebelian continue. With children living increasingly in urban contexts, this has become a priority for those whose work chimes with Froebelian education. In this chapter, a selection is made to illustrate some powerful examples of the ways in different parts of the world where Kindergarten trained Froebelians were determined in their efforts to ensure that gardens were part of the educational environment and were seen as ensuring outdoor learning in the deeper sense. They were not simply to be places for children to let off steam in between academic studies or to get fresh air or opportunities to play with a laissez faire lack of joining in from adults. Marjorie Ouvry points out that

> practitioners often feel confused about their role when they are outside, finding it difficult to decide whether they should be police constable, referee, observer, safety officer, assessor, arbitrator or instructor ... The quality of children's learning, the length of time they spend in exploration and the imagination within their play all increase if practitioners get involved, without dominating, and show that they are interested in what children are playing and exploring. (2001:82 and 83)

The following section gives examples of the way in which some of the early Kindergartens became attached to training colleges as they were established, which ensured that the trainee teachers saw Froebelian practice and did not just learn about it from books. They knew what to do when they spent time and taught the children in the garden and on visits to larger natural landscapes beyond.

Kindergartens attached to Kindergarten teacher training colleges

The Glory Kindergarten in Kobe, 1889

In 1889 Annie Howe, an American missionary, established the Glory Kindergarten in Kobe. This continues today. She had trained with Alice Putnam at the Chicago Froebel Association Training School (Prochner and Kirova, 2017:104). She worked to ensure that the Froebelian approach was not imposed on the Japanese cultural context, but instead demonstrated how it could chime with it (Nishida and Abe, 2017:157–67). The creation of a Kindergarten garden was central in this. Evidently children learnt their colours from the flowers, varying from violets to nasturtiums and roses, chrysanthemums, hydrangeas, pansies and wisteria. The Kindergarten played an important part in training Kindergarten teachers.

Rachel and Margaret McMillan

In England and Scotland, at the turn of the nineteenth century, nursery schools developed (a form of provision in Scotland and England pioneered by the Froebelian Margaret McMillan [1860–1931]) and were very often, having started as free schools or private schools, taken into the state sector to become maintained by local education authorities. Gardens, not playgrounds, remained part of this provision.

Some nursery schools led to the establishment of teacher training colleges, with which they remained linked, continuing to be involved in the training of the Kindergarten students. The nursery school in Deptford, founded by Margaret McMillan, who was an active member of the Froebel Society, is an example. The school came into being when she and her sister Rachel realized a need at the beginning of the First World War (1914–18). Her work in Bradford had already achieved the establishment of the School Medical Health and School Meal Service. The Rachel McMillan Nursery School founded in 1914 (named after her sister following her death) became linked to the Rachel McMillan Kindergarten Training College. Creating a garden as part of the classroom provision, together with the covered shelters extending from each classroom meant that children could spend time out of doors in all weathers. Parents working in the munitions' factory could help to grow vegetables and flowers which would encourage bees and birds. For example,

> Suppose you want to develop the touch sense! Lo! Here are a score of leaves, hairy sunflower, crinkled primrose, glossy fuchsia, and the rose. Do you want to compare colours, to note hues and shades? Well, here is wealth a plenty. The herb garden will offer more scents than anyone can put in a box, and very little thought will make of every pathway a riot of opportunities. (Bradburn, 1989:177)

Moray House nursery school, 1908 to 1988

Moray House nursery (established in 1908) in the University of Edinburgh did not have the extensive grounds for the study and participation in nature that was available to the Froebel Nursery Research School or the Redford House Nursery in the extensive Froebel College grounds. Nevertheless, the Froebelian essential of making it a central part of the curriculum prevailed. The garden was given great emphasis. It is much more challenging to ensure that children have opportunities to engage with nature in a densely populated urban context.

The Moray House nursery school transferred to a new purpose-built building in 1932. The last head, Margaret Cameron, continued training Kindergarten students at the Moray House College in the Froebelian approach until its closure through lack of funding in 1988. The garden surrounded the nursery and gave the children different levels to explore. The physical development of skills was part of the child's education in nature. Being active, digging, cutting and planting were all as important as running, jumping, hopping, skipping and climbing. In Chapter Five the Froebelian *Movement Games* are examined. These were often carried out in the garden in the early nursery schools, as early photographs show.

The Froebel Nursery Research School, 1972–7

The Froebel Nursery Research School was located in the grounds of the Froebel Educational Institute. Chris Athey was the research fellow and Tina Bruce was the head. Students from the college came for their teaching practices and visits. There were no fences around the garden. Children, aged from 2 to 5 years, played in the area outside the nursery building within the grounds and did not stray out of hearing. Parents were welcome to come with their children on the nursery's bus each day. There were rarely fewer than six parents accompanying the twenty children. The families lived on a large council housing estate in London, where playing outside was a challenge. Children could make dens in the bushes, climb trees and climbing frames. They could engage in gardening with the adults. There were also walks to the college lake, where tadpoles could be caught and returned to the habitat when frogs emerged. The grounds covered 350 acres (Weston, 1998), and so going for nature outings was something deeply valued by the families. Children learnt the names of flowers and trees, about the function of seeds and fruits, why bees matter, the names of water birds, and why different birds need different feet and beaks, and how different feathers work on bodies and wings. They also visited gardens like Kew gardens and Wimbledon Common.

Redford House Workplace Day Nursery, 1988–2010

A later example of a garden central to the Froebelian education is Redford House Workplace Day Nursery, established in 1988 and led by Lynne Bartholomew and her deputy, June Byne. Lynne also lectured in the college. This was linked to the training of early childhood students and teachers studying at what became the University of Roehampton. The building was part of the old stables located in the Froebel College grounds next to what was previously the Froebel Nursery Research School of the 1970s (Bruce, 2020:51). The garden was made of cobblestones with a large water pump donated by Principal Jill Redford, and was in constant use by the children. There were flower beds along the walls and trees providing shade. The children grew vegetables and flowers. As in the time of the Froebel Nursery Research School, small groups of children went for nature excursions with their key person in the grounds. These were active learning events. There are examples in the Lynne Bartholomew Collection, located in the Froebel Archive, University of Roehampton Library, with children making maps of their walks and drawing pictures of what they encountered.

Froebelian Child Gardens today

The a time-honoured tradition of Kindergartens in different parts of the world determinedly giving the garden a place of high value in the Froebelian approach is embraced. Felicity Thomas and Steph Harding, both headteachers, write about the observations they have made of children playing in the garden of the local-authority financed nursery school in Norfolk, where they have worked together over the years. According to Harding and Thomas:

> Our research over the years has found that the children respond to the garden joyously. The sand is a beach area where deep digging and burying could be experienced using whole body movement. Sand gives many different sensory experiences but having a deep sand area shows how cold sand can be on one's skin even in the very hottest weather and experience the weight of sand through burying oneself. The water is experienced in many different ways as it is in a pond, a rill (a manmade stream) with a water splash and a waterfall as it flows down the side of the magic mountain giving children the rich experience of how water can be found in nature.

> Throughout the years of the garden maturing we watched the children's learning and understanding about nature deepen. Looking through the many observations written we saw the children develop their creativity, often leading other children in their creative games and imaginings of "finding the dragon" or making houses for "The Three Little Pigs" so they will be safe from the wolf! One of our favourite days was the summer Solstice. This became Elves and Fairies day and everyone, children and adults dressed up as either an elf or a fairy. Each room learnt a traditional fairy tale and acted out this tale to each other and anyone else who was visiting. The children entered into the spirit of this day and the garden became a magical place. One year they made a fairy throne from living willow and this throne remained in the garden until both Steph and I left. Imagination was inspired, language developed, communication between all sparkled with the delight of these old stories. Children showed, persistence and determination and a love for storying. (Harding and Thomas, 2020:121–2)

Cowgate Under 5s Centre, Edinburgh

The garden experience is particularly difficult to achieve in a central city location such as Edinburgh. Cowgate Under 5s Centre is a current example of this being achieved. It is led by Dr Lynn McNair who is also a senior teaching fellow and lecturer for Early Childhood at the University of Edinburgh. The determination to provide a rich experience in the garden is evident in her writings and practice (McNair, 2012:57–69). The garden, following a carefully planned transformation developed soon after her appointment, is put to full use with climbing opportunities and flower beds with emphasis on growing and planting. Following her studies for the Froebel Certificate at the University of Roehampton in 2006, a consultation was undertaken with children, parents and staff. As a result, parents bought two fruit trees. Children responded saying:

'I want to look for spiders.' (Ailidh aged 4 years)

'I would like a pond with some tadpoles.' (Euan aged 3 years)

'I'd like a sandpit.' (Rosa aged 3 years)

(McNair, 2007:31)

So that children have opportunities for a larger area out of doors, every child has opportunities to spend uninterrupted time daily in the forest area near the centre for six weeks. According to McNair:

The children are 'learning through' and not just 'learning about' things such as fires, shelters or climbing trees. On returning to the centre we witness children learning how to negotiate steps, ramps, climb up and over large pieces of equipment in the garden and use real tools at the woodwork table. As a consequence we observe them developing into competent, risk aware rather than risk averse learners.

(2012:65).

Stella Brown points out that the early nursery schools were well described as 'Child Gardens':

Practitioners have the gift of nature to plan learning opportunities for young children in their long-term plan. To work through the certain effects and events of seasonal change, season by season, defining the labyrinth of learning opportunities and experiences within the garden provides staff, parents and children with a rich tapestry that is unaffected by other influences and conditions of life and events. There is a colourful kaleidoscope of meaningful, tangible, flexible and rich experiences that provide significant personal understanding and knowledge of life ... Respect for the power of nature, the potential for learning in the garden and recognising children's needs, stage of learning and understanding is paramount. (2012:38–9)

In one of the nursery schools, blackberry brambles are grown around the outside. This prevents intruders, but it also provides blackberries. Maureen Baker gives this example:

A group of children are involved in picking blackberries. They talk to each other and form theories about them. They are black. They are easy to squash. They grow on prickly brambles. You can eat them. You can cook them. They can make jam. They are using what they already know about blackberries from previous encounters with them and making links with what they now find. They might have eaten blackberry jam, but this is the first time they have been face-to-face with a blackberry before it turned into jam ... The boy who holds the basket keeps it still while other children drop blackberries into it. They are learning how to relate to each other with sensitivity, courteously and with co-operation. (Bruce, 2004:115)

These examples demonstrate the importance of training and participation in high quality Froebelian practice as key in both sustaining and disseminating the Froebelian approach to education. The Edinburgh Froebel Network is extending to other parts of Scotland. Gardens are promoted in a central way by this Froebelian Network. The Edinburgh Froebel Network was founded by Jane Whinnett and Lynn McNair with Maureen Baker, Stella Brown, Chris McCormick joined by Catriona Gill. As heads of Edinburgh City nursery schools, they established, working with the author of this book and Professor John Davis (then at the University of Edinburgh), a Froebel Certificate Course. This is now taught throughout Scotland, including Orkney and Shetland. The course links with the BA Early Childhood Studies course and the MSc with a Froebel pathway at the University of Edinburgh. Jane Read and Helen Tovey and the author teach this course. An important part of the course focuses on the garden. Chapter Eight looks in greater detail at the importance of Froebelian networks linked to the training of the next generation of Froebelians.

The Froebel Travelling Tutor Short Courses, endorsed by the Froebel Trust, are developing another important strand of Froebelian training in the UK. Of the five Elements 1–5, the garden is given an important place. The garden is introduced in Element one and is studied in greater depth in Element three. Several of the tutors were heads of local-authority financed nursery schools. For example, Steph Harding made careful observations of children involved in bike play in the garden:

In the interviews with the children there was a lot of evidence that speed was a major attraction of this activity. Three of the four said they liked the bikes because they 'go fast' and of those three, two said their favourite game on the bikes was 'going faster' and 'racing the bikes'. (Harding, 2001:39)

In Chapter Five there is consideration of Froebel's *Mother Play and Nursery Song*, about the weathervane on the roof of a church. There is a link with both bikes and nature here. Froebel is showing how nature is not always only seen. It is felt, as when the wind blows. The feeling of speed has some resonance here. The weather provides natural forces, and the way the human body moves (in this case on wheels) creates a different force with the air that surrounds us.

Kathryn Solly (2014), who was head of Chelsea Open Air Nursery School, in her book looking at risk, challenge and adventure in outdoor learning, distinguishes between what is dangerous and the importance of enabling environments which support children in risk taking.

Putting children to work in gardens and fields or giving children opportunities to engage with nature: A big difference

Earlier in this chapter, Jane Read contrasted the nineteenth-century gutter play of children with no gardens and the highly regulated gardens in free schools which removed them from street play. Froebel's response to the way that Pestalozzi prioritized teaching children of economically poor families how to work in agriculture developing their manual skills chimes with that of Margaret McMillan. Froebel felt that Pestalozzi spent too much time on mechanical instruction, instead of allowing the children to have and explore ideas about how to garden and farm. Froebel

> gave his schools gardens and landscapers far more romantic roles, envi-sioning them as not only settings for agricultural instruction, but sources for spiritual, cognitive and social development. (Herrington, 2001:30)

The Froebelian garden and landscape beyond are not simply utilitarian, and they are not classist. They are for all children, wherever they are in the world. Froebel criticizes Pestalozzi for over teaching in the field and garden with his insistence on doing things the proper way. But Froebel emphasized that children need opportunities to experiment, explore and discover. This may mean that at first they will give 'injurious treatment' to plants, but from seeing how the plants flourish in the communal garden that surrounds them, they begin to work out what to do so that it makes sense to them, and they actively choose the way that makes the plants grow well. They see adults working in the communal garden and learn from this. Froebel wants children to learn how to garden and farm, but in ways which are at the right time, in the right way for them. *Freedom with guidance* is a recurring theme in Froebelian education.

Herrington (2001; 1998) points out that with the shift from agricultural lifestyles to small-town developments in the United States as the twentieth century developed, many schools and Kindergartens abandoned gardens as part of the provision. Instead, they introduced playgrounds. Elizabeth

Peabody was an exception, in visiting the German Kindergartens where she saw gardens provided by Kindergarten teachers who had trained with Froebel or the first wave of practitioners trained in Keilhau. The Froebelian garden was changed in the translation into the American context (Prochner, 2017:7). She saw the value of the garden and made it an important part of the Kindergarten education in Boston. She was struggling against a tidal wave in this respect. Susan Blow, working in St Louis took a different view, changing the original vision so that the garden was dropped, while at the same time requiring a rigid adherence to the exact replication of the use of the *Gifts* and *Occupations*:

> Kindergartens succeeded in name only in the modern American educational system because many of their romantic tendencies, like the symbolic gardens and contemplative excursions, were reinvented or simply dropped. Kindergartens in England, the Netherlands, and Japan, still maintained some gardening and nature study programs. (Hetherington, 2001:44)

The influence of Dewey (1859–1952) was becoming strong in the United States, and this undermined the importance of the Froebelian garden and wilder landscapes beyond. He considered Froebel's thinking to be Romantic and instead focused on the vocabulary and scientific learning that could be achieved through gardening. Like Pestalozzi, he regulated the way that children spent time exploring nature, gardening and playing:

> Dewey disregarded the symbolic imagery of the kindergarten garden culture … Dewey's approach dissected and classified nature into a digestible system for memorization … which contrasted with that of Froebel who stressed the revelatory powers of these excursions. (Herrington, 2001:43)

Dewey linked the garden and the classroom through the science of cookery. Like Pestalozzi he separated the different subjects. In the Froebelian Kindergarten this was not so. Children would certainly learn the science, but there would also be emphasis on: the meal preparation; the presentation of the food; who would gather flowers from the garden for the centre of the table; who would sit where; who would serve at the table; and clear away; and the enjoyable conversations taking place when sharing the meal together. Language would flow. Vocabulary would expand, and as the gardening image says, children would come to *know their onions* – but in their own time, and in their own way, through the help of the adults giving *freedom with guidance*. However, Dewey felt that,

Cooking gives opportunity for getting a great many ideas of heat and water, and their effects. The scientific work taken up in the school differs mainly from that of other schools in having the experimental part – physics and chemistry – emphasised, and is not confined simply to nature study, but we find it possible to introduce the physical aspects from the first. (1990:174)

The continuation of Froebelian gardens and adventures in nature landscapes beyond

Gardening is a constant process and needs maintenance. With issues of climate change, and the mental and physical health of children, concerns about fresh air and fading contact with nature, there is a sense of urgency from present-day Froebelians to ensure the survival of gardens in schools and day-care settings. Jane Dyke, writing of the thirteen Yellow Dot day nurseries, says:

We are lucky enough to have reasonable sized gardens, so we immediately started to observe what was actually happening within them. What we found was that we had a surprising amount of fairly boring plastic toys that were not well utilised (interestingly no-one could remember buying them). We also found that we spent quite a bit of time 'setting up' the gardens each day and then packing away. On reflection, this was because much of the equipment and toys that we had were not outdoor friendly and so had to be stored. Following these observations, we decided to declutter our gardens using the 'less is more' principle. We tried to take everything out of the gardens that did not really belong in a garden. Out ultimate aim was not to have to set up the garden but instead to have a garden that is natural and/or outdoor friendly. (Dyke in Bruce and Dyke, 2017d:24)

The children now regularly go on adventures into the wider landscape beyond the garden of the nursery. Sometimes the children go into the forest, and sometimes they visit local places that involve walking:

We have engaged with our local Forest Schools and developed our own Nature Nursery, where we bus our children to spend the whole day 'playing in nature' … Froebel has opened up the outdoors to us and it has now become a rich learning environment that is developing with the seasons … Slowly over time we have become less attached to our 'walking rings' and when appropriate, we are now walking alongside our children and interacting as family, rather than as regiments.

(Dyke, 2017:25)

The Froebelian garden and the wilder landscapes beyond have been subjected to historic and cultural influences since they were first conceived by Froebel. Much of the original thinking that Froebel did in designing the gardens and thinking about the excursions into the countryside has been lost. It is time to unearth what has been buried and to ensure that children, helped and in partnership with the adults who spend time with them, understand and act together in the importance of the earth which is our planet on which our survival depends. According to Froebel,

> Many adults as well as children treat Nature as one ordinarily treats the air: one lives in it while knowing almost nothing about it ... if he does not find the same awareness among adults the seed of knowledge just beginning to germinate within him is crushed. He rightly requires adults to confirm his perceptions, and if this does not happen he suppresses his original feelings. (Froebel in Lilley, 1967:146)

The children

In the Annan School, East Sussex, which strives to be Froebelian, there is a garden, but there are also wider forests and fields abutting. The children in the Kindergarten each took a piece of ground under the trees and made miniature worlds. There were roads made from pebbles and houses made from tree bark. People were put together, using sticks and string, with clothes of leaves and flower petals. The people could drink from acorn cups and eat from plates of shells. They went to bed covered in moss duvets. Their pillows were made of wool the children had found on excursions in the fields, caught on bushes. Fences between fields were plaited with bendy twigs. Trees made of feathers were made to stand in rows. There were lakes and rivers, using tin foil to keep the water in. There were boats of tree bark. Froebel believed that the garden and landscapes beyond should, would, lead to the burgeoning of the *symbolic life*. The children used their knowledge of nature to find their props. There was plenty of discussion as they went about making their miniature worlds such as finding oak trees, because underneath would be the acorns and their cups. They gave each other tips, or showed them how to plait, weave, use string to keep the clothes on the stick dolls. Knowing about nature was part of this. It was physical too. Stepping carefully to the far side of the scenario, placing the props so that they were not damaged were important considerations.

These children, Segun and Joan, are being encouraged by their families at home and in the local park respectively, to engage with nature from babyhood (Froebel, 1912:240). Segun, who is 2 years old, had been helping his parents to water the tomato plant on the balcony. He saw the tomatoes beginning to grow and turn from green to red. He helped to pick them, and they ate them for supper.

Joan is 8 months old. She is outside and has been placed on a mat on the grass. She is just beginning to crawl. Near the mat is a log and on the other side is a garden chair. With huge effort she manages to crawl to the log, and to heave herself up. She clearly wants to climb the log. Her mother brings the chair across so that she can stand up, leaning against it. But she likes the log. She crawls off the mat, and round to the circular cut off part of the trunk of the tree. She keeps fingering the rough circles, not tracing them, but enjoying the way bits stick out. Within her physical capabilities she is risk taking. Her mother knows that and dare not leave her company, but she does leave her to explore. Froebel felt that:

Throughout his childhood he should be allowed to maintain this connection with Nature and its phenomena as a focus of his life, and this is done mainly through the encouragement of his play which at first is only natural life. (Froebel in Lilley, 1967:83)

CHAPTER FOUR

Play, Imagination, Creativity and the *Symbolic Life* of the Child

There has been a muddled use of the word 'play' by politicians, academics, researchers, parents, those who train practitioners, set examinations and assess accredited courses and even the practitioners themselves. Play remains impossible to pin down, and is not open to measurement (Brehony, 2017:27) or definition. It is against this background that the difficult task exists of trying to tease out what constitutes a Froebelian approach to play. The elusiveness of what play might be in general terms, and what it is in specifically Froebelian terms chimes with the poem by Xenophanes:

> The gods did not reveal from the beginning
> All things to us; in the course of time
> Through seeking, men find that which is the better.
> But as for certain truth, no man has known it,
> Nor will he know it; neither of the gods,
> Not yet of all things of which I speak.
> And even if by chance he were to utter
> The final truth, he would himself not know it;
> For all is but a woven web of guesses. (Xenophanes (c. 570–475 BCE)

Froebel is the educator whose name has probably become the most closely linked with promoting play as an important part of early childhood education. At times in history, and in different parts of the world, play has come to be regarded as a making a major contribution to the improvement of education and to the lives of young children. At other times, and in different places, the inclusion of play in the early childhood curriculum has been seen by some educators, academics and politicians as a waste of precious educational opportunities. There have been a number of challenges, each leading to the situation in which Froebelian play is located today. After Froebel's death in 1852 and the scattering of his trainees and supporters with the issue of the Verbot closing his schools and the training of Kindergarten teachers in Saxony, different interpretations of his approach inevitably emerged. Some advocates, like Susan Blow in the United States and Bertha Ronge in England, stayed close to the tangible aspects, focusing on a rigid interpretation of the *Gifts* and *Occupations*. The outdoors was neglected and almost lost. Others became influenced by the emerging sciences. This meant moving away from the *Gifts* and *Occupations, Mother Songs* and *Movement Games*. They were either abandoned or transformed and adapted to fit the new sciences. The new practitioners

> insisted that although Froebel's methods were outdated, the underlying principles of his work had permanent value. Seen in this light, Froebel's ideas could be seen as compatible with the newer, more scientific educational methods that the Froebel Society wholly embraced. (Nawrotzki, 2019:62)

By the 1930s, the invasion of science resulted in the disappearance of the original Froebelian materials used in the way that they had been designed. Kevin Brehony's (2017:27) warning that Froebelians should take care not to fall into the trap of positivism is important to heed. As the twentieth century developed, the Child Study Movement and the scientific focus of the laboratory schools in American universities century made this a real issue. By the 1960s, in the UK, to suggest that reading Froebel's writings in a serious way, that went beyond learning history, with an aim to practically engage with how he did things was out of the question. His actual practices were regarded as obsolete and his language arcane. There was also challenge from a group of philosophers (Richard Stanley Peters, Paul Hirst, Robert F. Dearden) who, engaging in conceptual analysis, critiqued the concept of play and cast doubts on its contribution to education. Dearden found 'A still continuing child-centred tradition of eulogising play' (1968:94).

This 'regime of truth' (Foucault, 1980) continues today, but is being eroded by reconnecting Froebelians. The principles linked with the original practices of Froebel are being seriously explored. Froebelian principles and practices are being reconnected in important ways which are beneficial to early childhood education. Froebelian training is being transformed in the process. As is usually the case with strategic changes (Ian Bruce, 2013), transformational changes come from the grassroots and work their way upward. Practitioners working in the UK, South Africa, Kolkata, Australia and Japan (Bruce, Elfer and Powell, 2019) for example, are reporting that they are finding Froebel's language is far from arcane in relation to the concept of play. The Froebelian vocabulary encapsulates in simple forms the essence of important messages for the way practitioners want to work in their worlds, in their cultures, today. They are exploring the original *Gifts* and *Occupations, Mother Songs and Movement Games,* and his thinking about *Nature* and outdoor learning.

Froebel's journey: The realization of the importance of play in childhood

It is often impossible to pinpoint exactly how and when important concepts come to fruition. This is certainly the case when examining Froebel's understanding and promotion of play in the education of young children. As a child he spent long hours in the garden, alone. Later, he spent time alone in the forest. When he pondered on the essence of play later, he was able to distinguish between the value of solitary play and the state of loneliness. His time in Pestalozzi's school led him to build on his childhood first-hand experiences and *Engagement with Nature.* Observing the younger children in Yverdun, he recognized that they were struggling with the way they were required to learn about real objects. This made him think. After leaving Pestalozzi's school in Yverdun, Switzerland, he began observing children at play and from 1818 the value of discussing what he saw with his colleagues and wife Wilhelmine Henriette in Keilhau would have helped to bring to fruition his *Gifts* and *Occupations, Mother Songs* and *Movement Games.* Each of them, in different ways, are tangible elements of his thinking about the importance of childhood play and emerged through careful observation, pilot work and evaluation as part of a constant state of becoming.

He deeply appreciated the love and nurture he received as a boy in his maternal uncle's home, where he began to meet boys of his age and to go on adventures in the countryside. The contrast with being alone, earlier in his father's house, would have contributed to his thinking about being in a collaborative context. Helping each other to cross the stream is a more satisfying group experience than taunting those who are left behind. The *Movement Games* reflect this kind of thinking, beginning with the child moving alone in a song or game but then in collaboration with others in a group dance or song. Children are free to modify and alter the games and to make them their own. Through his observations, Froebel had seen that although children might get together and use a song as it was designed in the first instance, once the group participants became comfortable with each other, they would deviate more from the set pieces and make them their own. This is something also noted by the Opies (Opie and Opie, 1980), who gathered the singing games of children playing in the street.

By 1826, Froebel's book *The Education of Man* was published. In this, his thinking about play is signalled. His thoughts on this subject had been maturing over some time. As always there is absolute consistency in his approach. Lilley (1967:3) writes about the difficulties of Froebel's writing style and suspects that very few educators read the book in its entirety. Lilley sees his writings in letters, pamphlets and in this, his most major writing, as being the ways in which he developed and elaborated his thoughts and appealed for support and help. But although the writing features outpourings, when it comes to looking at what he says about play, they are remarkably consistent and show a clear line of developing thinking. It is well worth the effort of unpicking what he is thinking. According to Froebel:

> Play is the highest level of child development. It is the spontaneous expression of thought and feeling – an expression which his inner life requires. This is the meaning of the word 'play'. It is the purest creation of the child's mind as it is also a pattern and copy of the natural life hidden in man and in all things. So it promotes enjoyment, satisfaction, serenity, and constitutes the source of all that can benefit the child. A child who plays well of his own accord, quietly persisting until he is physically tired out, will develop as an efficient and determined person, ever ready to make sacrifices for the good of himself and others. This age has no lovelier sight than that of a child absorbed in play, so completely absorbed that eventually he falls asleep as he plays.

> At this age play is never trivial; it is serious and deeply significant. It needs to be cherished and encouraged by the parents, for in his free choice of play a child reveals the future life of his mind to anyone who has insight into human nature. (Froebel in Lilley, 1967:83–4)

Froebel has captured the essence of his approach to play. He gives play status in the home, but also values it because of the way it contributes to the child's education. It really is an educational basic in his thinking. This is because it reveals the future life of the mind. It is once again a demonstration of his belief in the state of becoming that occurs though life. This chimes with the thinking of later theorists such as Eric H. Erikson and Lev Vygotsky (Bruce, 1991:32; Vygotsky, 1978). Erikson sees the third of his eight stages of life as the time when children play and pretend. This is typically from 4 to 6 years of age. Through play, Erikson sees children developing initiative and becoming equipped to deal with disappointment, and to approach life with a sense of increasingly focused purpose. Children are always in partnership with their futures. Vygotsky made a famous statement about play, which resonates with Froebel's belief that it should be given the highest status because it is a leading factor in educational development:

> In play a child always behaves beyond his average age, above his daily behaviour; in play it is as though he were a head taller than himself. As in the focus of a magnifying glass, play contains all developmental tendencies in a condensed form and is itself a major source of development. (Vygotsky, 1978:102)

Froebel saw the education of the child as a journey from the sensory experiences and the literal to increasingly abstract ways of thinking through the emerging and developing *symbolic life*. In this respect Donald W. Winnicott's work (Winnicott, 1974; Bruce, 2015:110) chimes with Froebel's *Mother Play and Nursery Songs* (1844) and *Mother Songs, Games and Stories* (1895). Winnicott developed the concept of the transitional object. The child has an object which gives comfort in the absence of parent, but which also begins to take on an imaginative life. Froebel, through his observations, realized that objects are important to children as they play, but it is not known to what extent he discussed with parents the way in which children use their loved objects to express their feelings, relationships and ideas as they play. With only a little encouragement from adults or older children, their fingers transform into characters and become people, or bees, birds, fish from nature or objects such as a table. Froebel's writings give hints about the pleasure children take in play. He calls these *Finger Plays*. For example, he writes of the *Mother Songs*, 'Even his own fingers must become something else such as fishes or birds' (Lilley, 1967:112). The point here is the understanding that Froebel has of the journey from sensory experiences, to literal understandings and then the transformative use by the child of more abstract thinking and ideas. The question that arises is: How do children begin to use their fingers symbolically? Do they always do this spontaneously? Do adults need to show them the possibilities? Is it different with different children?

The educational value of play

Play has high status in Froebelian education. But although it is seen as desirable to promote it, there is also the recognition that children cannot be made to play. Offering gold stars, stickers or other kinds of extrinsic reward and inducement is alien to Froebelian education in relation to play or any aspect of the approach. Instead, self-discipline and intrinsic motivation are developed (Bruce and Dyke, 2017f). Play feeds this *inner life*. Play helps children to understand and deal with what are often challenging situations which require thinking about the world they inhabit inside themselves, and the world they live in external to themselves. The relationship and connection making the *inner outer* and the *outer inner* brings understanding of self, in relation to others and the universe of nature and the peopled world. *Unity* is fundamental to grasping the essence of Froebelian play. The child who perseveres when trying to fasten the baby doll's jacket is motivated from within to see something through, even though it involves struggle. Although play creates a pretend world, it echoes real life in many ways. Froebel suggests that the reality might be hidden in the play, but it is there. Froebel recognizes that the child absorbed in play strives to participate in real life. It is the core to the future.

Arguments about the place of play in education both then and now cluster around the role of the adult. Adults are surely Froebelian when they encourage children to think for themselves, to be aware of themselves and their ideas, feelings and relationships, and to nurture what is *inner* be expressed in *outer* ways through imaginative and creative use of the *Gifts, Occupations, Finger Plays* and *Movement Games* and in *Nature*. Looking at childhood play in isolation, it is easy to miss the more subtle and sophisticated hints and messages that Froebel gives in the array of writings he has left behind as his legacy. It is when the interconnected whole, the *Unity* in what he says is explored that his interactionist stance can be seen. The *Forms* of *everyday life, Beauty,* and *Knowledge; freedom with guidance; self-activity* of the child, *symbolic life* of the child, relationship of the *inner and outer*, and the *law of opposites* are important points of access into his approach to childhood play. These help us, in the world of today, to implement with integrity a Froebelian approach to play. We can then make interactive and connected Froebelian use of the *Mother Songs, Movement Games, Gifts* and *Occupations* and *Engagement with Nature*.

The dark side of play

It can be argued that Froebel takes what Dearden might see as a eulogized view of play. Kevin Brehony (2017:16) raises the issue of the dark side of play, and the way adults, fearing that children might become subversive, disorderly and transgressive in their play, close it down and prevent it. Froebel recognized that play, when it flows, allows children to deal with forces of both good and evil. By playing at being a 'baddy', the child does not become bad. It is a powerful way of seeing the consequences of different actions, but in a way that is safe from reality. In play, a child

> positively seeks that which is best for himself – though he may do so unconsciously – in a form appropriate to his abilities and means. (Froebel in Lilley, 1967:51)

It might be appropriate to be a 'baddy' and to experiment with evil. For Froebel:

> The child who seems rude and self -willed is often involved in an intense struggle to realise the good by his own effort. (Froebel in Lilley, 1967:51)

He goes on to say:

Children are able to make fine and accurate distinctions between those requests which are personal and arbitrary and those which are expressions of general imperatives. (Froebel in Lilley, 1967:56)

When children are in a state of 'free-flow play', either alone or in a group, they are engaging in Froebel's 'expressions of general imperatives'. They make a distinction between what is real life and real life in playing. They are teasing out the interconnectivity of the *inner* and the *outer*. Children are free to express themselves in their play, but they are also 'part of the circle of life'. This is not free expression or a laissez-faire approach to childhood play. According to Froebel,

The child's need to make use of the most pliable and delicate material in his creative work is in accordance with the activity and phenomena of Nature which creates from light, air, water earth and dust ... . We must respect the child's desire to affirm his powers of expression through these objects, since he is proving that he is both a creative being and also a part of the whole circle of life. (Froebel in Lilley, 1967:115)

Freedom with guidance: An interactionist approach to play

Froebel valued *freedom with guidance* and this implies a much more interactionist approach than mere self-expression. One of the challenges in exploring Froebelian play and what it looks like is the writings of those Froebelians who promoted Froebelian education after his death. Revisionist Froebelians emphasized free expression as being at the heart of play. Others took a different direction. Brehony (2017:17) points out that Froebelians interpreting Froebel at the turn of the twentieth century often saw play as the child's work. Examples would be Eleonore Heerwart, Froebel's nephew Karl, Susan Blow or the influential Baroness von Marenholtz-Bulow, who saw play as a vehicle through handwork and exercises towards building a good work ethic. Another example would be the Kindergarten in Otago in New Zealand, which promoted weaving as a key *Occupation*, but it was very formally taught (May, 2017:176). These Froebelians supported guided play or play tutoring. On the surface, these examples of founders of Kindergartens do not appear to encourage children to play freely. In fact, it seems more likely, returning to the original writings of Froebel, rather than the interpretations by those following after his death, that he was more of an interactionist (Bruce, 1987; 2020). Hence, throughout his writings there is an emphasis on *freedom with guidance*. In Chapter Seven, his thinking on the importance of observation is explored, and this also helps in forming a view of how he approached play. He consistently emphasizes the importance of observation as a powerful way of understanding how to tune into where the child is, in terms of their thinking and their play. He wanted children to engage in thinking as a crucial part of their education. He also wanted them to enjoy their learning, although he did embrace the importance of struggle as a part of learning. Play cannot be the highest form of learning if it leaves out the need to think. Throughout his writings, in letters and publications, Froebel makes clear his belief that helping children to think is at the core of education. When the play is rich, so is the thinking. It reveals the child's future mind.

Free play or interactionist play

Whether it should be left to children to indulge in free play, or for adults to guide and tutor the play are matters that have been long debated. The former tends towards the therapeutic value of play, and the latter leads to learning outcomes and goals achieved. Neither seem to be Froebelian. It looks as if Froebel's approach to play was interactionist neither laissez-faire nor using the transmission model of instruction (Bruce 1991; 1996; 2020).

If, in reality, Froebel saw play more in the spirit of a conversation with a child than an opportunity for instruction, then it is quite natural for the adult to begin the conversation at times. Singing a *Finger Play* with the baby or toddler on the adult knee might start the conversation. Often children will be creative in their replies. He is very consistent in noting that he is very comfortable about things changing in the light of a child's taking control and using initiative. He says of the *Movement Games* that although he always begins with a simple game involving a ball, he is happy for children to change the game and to be expressive, innovative, imaginative and creative in the way they respond. Words in his writings and letters such as 'cramped', 'hindered' and 'spontaneous' are important clues that children have a say in an interactionist approach to play. Sometimes children begin to initiate play, and sometimes adults trigger it. This is *freedom with guidance*. As is clear in his letter,

> It is not at all needful to follow the order of the games as given in a series. This would quite destroy that fresh, merry life which should animate the games. One rule must be observed; the games must always begin with the easiest and limit free choice and unhindered play of movement is allowed. Otherwise the games would cease to be games and would lose their full educational power. You yourself, dear cousin, like every game-leader, would find yourself cramped and hindered. The freer and more

spontaneous the arrangement the more excellent is the effect. (Froebel letter IV to Murray, 1929:11)

This give-and-take approach between child and adult offers another perspective in relation to his concept of *freedom with guidance,* which threads through his work. In the letter just quoted, he does not emerge as laissez-faire, or as advocating a transmission model of instruction in relation to play. Once again he seems to be an interactionist (Bruce, 1987; 1991; 2020). As Froebel says:

If he is building a house, he builds it so that he can live in it as grown-up people do, so that he can have his own cupboard and so on, and be able to give them something out of it. One should be careful not to give a child the sort of gift which will overwhelm him, for it is important that he should be able to give something in return, In fact, it is necessary for him to do so, and he is happy when he knows how to meet this need by various things he can give away. (Froebel in Lilley, 1967:38)

Spontaneous play is in evidence, but the child is pleased to have a supportive adult nearby. The Kindergarten he invented is a place so arranged that play is included in the education of young children:

Little children, especially those under school age, ought not to be *schooled* and taught, they need merely to be *developed*. (Froebel from a letter to Ida Seele, March 14th, 1847, in Murray, 1929:27, emphasis in the original)

Froebel has been described as taking a laissez-faire and Romantic approach to childhood play. This seems to be unlikely on investigating the way he developed and used the *Gifts* and *Occupations* or the *Mother Songs* and *Movement Games.* He did not leave children alone in the garden, but he knew how and when to help (Figure 4.1). This was informed by his observations which became increasingly informed across time. This is not a laissez-faire approach. He did not give children adult set tasks for their play. He did not invade their play.

The symbolic life of the child: Play, imagination and creativity

In their play children build dens, especially in the garden, forest or countryside. This involves scientific knowledge about engineering constructions, skill relating to their physical development and social interactions as they work together and learn through each other (Liebschner, 1985). The look of the den brings in an artistic aspect. They create stories, with characters

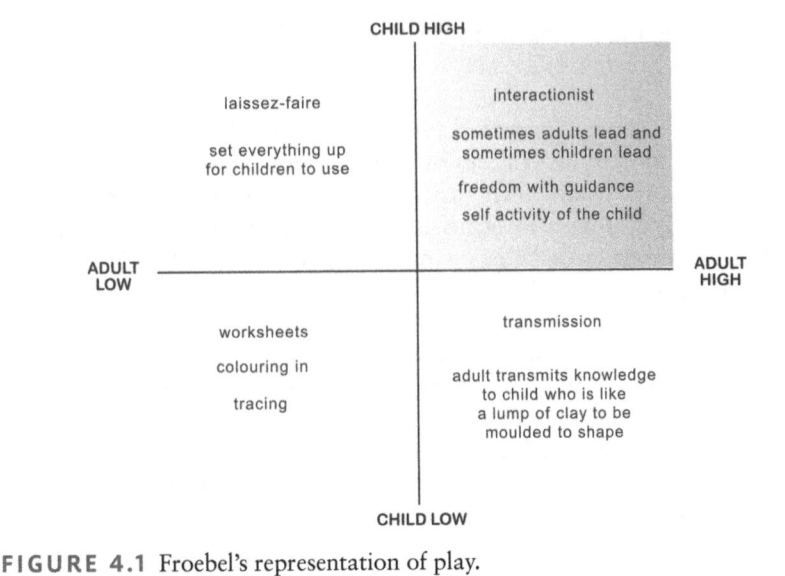

FIGURE 4.1 Froebel's representation of play.

Note: The shaded area represents Froebel's interactionist approach to play which requires high engagement from both children and adults.

inhabiting the den. They are influenced by the geography, history and culture of where they live in the world. Everything is linked in Froebelian education. Here the *Forms* of *Everyday life, Beauty and Knowledge* are evident and interconnected.

Froebel's way of encouraging parents and teachers to help children think for themselves so that they become active, creative, reflective and autonomous learners and are helped to do so through their play was revolutionary then and remains so now in most parts of the world. This kind of education avoids automatic acceptance and reliance on traditional thinking or the voices of authority figures or organizations. Froebel placed helping children to think at the centre of his educational approach. He gave play high status because it brings about thinking that is socially orientated, helps self-awareness, helps the literal to become more abstract, and ponders on and strives for harmony, symmetry and beauty. It is unlikely that he would have given such time, effort and place to the importance of play if it did not meet his requirement that children need to be supported to develop their thinking. This is why family life matters. This is what Kindergartens and schools are for.

The twelve features of 'free-flow play' (Bruce, 1991; 1996; 2015; 2017; 2020) arose from exploration of Froebel's thinking. They chime with current research about play, but this is not the dominant or leading influence. The aim is to reconnect Froebelian principles with original Froebelian practices in ways fit for worthwhile educational purposes in different parts of the world, but which have Froebelian authenticity. There is emphasis on the importance of first-hand experiences and this links to the Froebelian *Forms* and the *self-activity* of the child. The *symbolic life of the child* is given status through the emphasis on pretending and creating other worlds. In play, control is given to children to competently and freely apply what they know in innovative creative and imaginative ways. That adults are able to join the play, providing they understand the concept of *freedom with guidance* is key to understanding Froebelian play. There is a valuing of solitary play, which gives opportunities for children to become self-aware, and to understand themselves. Through knowing themselves, children relate to others and to the world out there. This embraces the concept of *Unity* which involves the relationship and processes of flowing and becoming through the making of the *inner outer and the outer inner* and exploration of *opposites* which Froebel called the *spherical law* (Liebschner, [1992]2001:8). The group play engages children in teasing out the *law of opposites* as they explore good and evil, kindness and brutality, lack of forgivingness or redemption, justice or lack of it and so much more, such as giving and kindness.

1. Play actively uses previous first-hand experiences, including the playing out of struggle, physical activity, exploration, discovery and trying out what has been learnt.

2. It exerts no pressure to conform to rules, pressures, goals, tasks or definite direction. It enables experimentation with rules.

3. It is an active process without a product. Any product fades when the play ends.

4. It is intrinsically motivated. Children cannot be made to play.

5. It is about possible, alternative worlds, involves pretending and lifts players to their highest levels of functioning. This involves being imaginative, creative, original and innovative.

6. It is about participants wallowing in ideas, feelings and relationships. It involves reflecting on and becoming aware of what we know.

7. Play is sustained and when in full flow, helps children to function in advance of what they can actually do in their real lives.

8. During free flow play, children use the technical prowess, mastery and competence they have previously developed. They are in control.

9. Play can be initiated by the child or by an adult, but if initiation is by the adult, they must be sensitive to the other players and avoid exerting pressure on children to conform to their adult agenda.

10. Play can be solitary.

11. It can be in partnerships, groups with adults and children sensitively playing together.

12. Play is an integrating mechanism. It brings together everything we learn, know, feel and understand.

(Bruce, 1991; 2020)

At the heart of his approach to play is Froebel's belief that children, through the tangible, are able to move to increasingly abstract ways of thinking. The *Forms*, surface again. *Everyday life* appears first in play, from the manipulation of object with hand, eye and mouth coordination, to being literally used at first, typically playing at bedtime and food preparation scenarios such as the mechanics of physical prowess, leadership of a team, knowing the steps necessary to drive a car or comforting a baby. The way play drives children to find *Unity* so that there is completion through seeking the harmony and patterns of *Beauty* through teasing out solutions is present. Through 'free-flow play' children are able to apply *Knowledge* of a number of subjects and situations, such as making a map using wooden blocks to show how to get from their home to grandma's home. As the *symbolic life* becomes strengthened through play, children learn through and with each other, supported by the adult who is sensitive to their ideas and feelings. The play moves from literal to abstract, pretending to live on the moon, under the sea, in a fairy castle, in old-fashioned days, on a farm, or in a war, as a robot, or a dog, cat, baby. Milda Bredikyte (2017:4) sees this as mature play. The process of becoming and the concept of *Unity* are part of the deepening of the application of knowledge acquired by children. Play has an important contribution to make in bringing this about.

Children at play in the home context

Alex is 9 months old. He is sitting on the floor, with a colander full of potatoes for peeling. He concentrates intently, trying to pick them up one at a time. He uses both hands because some are too large to lift with one hand. But he can lift the smaller ones with one hand. It might look as if he is playing alone, and that this is child-initiated play. But it is interactionist. The adult decided to place the materials on the floor for him to play with. The choice of materials was that of the adult. Although the adult was preparing the meal, peeling potatoes at the table, she was with him, interested in what he was doing, near but far. He felt safe and secure enough to wallow and relax into his play. There is *freedom with guidance,* The *Forms* of *Everyday life* and *Beauty* are there, as part of food preparation. He is acquiring *Knowledge* about *Nature* indirectly, but it is knowledge of an important kind, as the potatoes come from the garden. He is using the *law of opposites*, as some potatoes are big and small much smaller. He demonstrates his mastery in picking up objects of different sizes. No one is making him play. This is *self-activity*. There is an intermingling here of Froebel's writings on play and the twelve features of play (Bruce, 1991; 2020).

Sofia and Lawry are both 2-years-olds. They are introduced to a set of unit blocks, a modern version of Froebel's *Gifts*. Lawry immediately begins to use them and builds a road with a building that is very tall. He talks as he does so, telling his uncle what he is doing. Sofia observes them from across the room and, after a while, comes to use the blocks. She does not join in with them, but quietly builds her own construction, which is very symmetrical and involves balancing blocks at interesting angles. The *Form* of *Everyday life* is here. The children live in a town and have both chosen to represent buildings, one with a running commentary and the other with a quiet, concise statement. Although nothing is said about the *Beauty* of their constructions, they are just beautiful, and seeing things that have symmetry or interesting angles seeps into people from a young age. There is *self-activity* with an atmosphere of encouraging adults, who do not overwhelm with too much interest, but are pleased to be with the children. The children sense that. It means that the *inner life, the symbolic life,* has the conditions that are conducive to it becoming *outer*. The play can flow and keeps moving so that the constructions keep changing. There is balancing, rearranging, matching, contrasting (*the law of opposites)* and mastery.

Lila is 4 years old. Her grandmother buys a small heather plant to give her parents when they are out shopping together. She loves the plant. At home she decides to call it 'Planty'. She sits it on a doll's chair. She gives it meals with a spoon. She takes it for walks in the pram. *The symbolic life* dominates in this play, and she shows that she can move a long way from the literal to more abstract ideas about characters and narratives. She relishes it. She is playing with play (Athey, 1990). Froebel's *Form* of *Everyday life* is there. Planty does everyday things, such as eating and going out in the pram.

Jacob is 3 years old. He plays with a set of cars at home. He makes engine noises and parks the cars. He goes into reverse. He stops at traffic lights. He uses the satellite navigation. His knowledge of cars is evident. He understands what gears are for, and brakes. He knows it is difficult to find parking spaces but needs to so that he can talk on the mobile phone. Here is Froebel's statement that play is a 'copy of the natural life hidden in man and in all things'. Jacob lives in a town and is demonstrating how much he knows about getting about as part of his daily life.

Donny is 8 years old. He goes to school on a school bus, and joins his class for sports, gymnastics, art and music. He works with a specialist teacher for other aspects of his education. When he gets home, he is tired, hungry and grumpy after being cooped up and sitting still on the school bus. His teacher makes a home visit and asks Donny's mother to help him enact a story of getting home after school. The teacher pretends to be a child who is cross and grumpy. Donny is shocked and highly critical of this story. He wants the teacher to act it out again, but this time asks him to be 'nice to my

Mum'. They do the scene again. This leads to discussion about how people feel when people are cross and grumpy with them when, in fact, they could have a nice time making tea together and enjoying each other's company. He wants to play this every day on return from school for several days. In this play scenario the Froebelian *Forms* are evident. *Everyday* situations are the content. Social rather than visual harmony is explored *(Beauty)*. Donny is helped through his play to bring to the surface what he in fact knows. Being grumpy is unfair, and it is much more enjoyable and harmonious in life to make the effort to overcome this by helping to make tea and chatting together over a meal. The play helps him to make this *Knowledge* become tangible. The play is literal at one level, but by being so it gives access to the more abstract – the effort of overcoming tiredness and hunger so that family can enjoy coming together.

Stevie is 6 years old. She has been given some large beads for her birthday. She arranges them in a circle and pretends they are children at school. She decides one is the teacher. The teacher is firm and clear and full of authority. Not to be argued with. She gives different beads different characters. They all have different voices. They are going to watch a show, and she fetches a torch to make stage lights. Her younger sister, Lila joins her. The plot becomes more complex, accommodating the ideas of both children, with give and take as they negotiate. Lila does a great deal of 'managing up', possibly because she knows from past experience that this will keep the play flowing. If she does not, things could become tricky and the play would halt. Stevie knows this too and tries to introduce things into the play that her sister will enjoy, such as being the person who switches the lights on and off during the show. Here, in the play, are the future challenges of leadership, managing a team, being in a team, being managed and learning how to manage your boss. As Froebel points out:

> Play is to the child a mirror of life -long struggles that await him. Therefore in order to gain strength for these, children seek obstacles, difficulties and strife in their play.
>
> (Froebel, 1826:118)

CHAPTER FIVE

Finger Plays, Mother Songs and Movement Games

Froebel, across the years, made a philosophical journey starting with a focus on children in the middle years of childhood in his school in Keilhau (1817). Without abandoning this age group, he then moved to thinking about the younger children from about 2 to 7 years, which led to his invention of the Kindergarten in Blankenburg (1837–40). It was in the last part of his journey that he focused on the education of babies and toddlers when he developed the *Mother Play and Nursery Songs* (1844), (*Mutter und Koselieder*). Reaching backwards to the beginnings of childhood, he sustained his exploration of the importance of interconnectivity. The *Mother Songs*, with the emphasis on the connections within whole body, limbs, hands and fingers, transition into *Movement Games* for children who walk, talk and pretend. As always, his thinking results in a nuanced and layered approach to education which was sophisticated and subtle. The *Finger Plays* in the *Mutter und Koselieder* fascinate babies, but also bring enjoyment and different kinds of educational value to the whole family and connect to carers and Kindergarten practitioners. For the babies they offered music, language in poetry and pictures with appropriate interactive physical play. For the siblings and family of the baby there is the joy of seeing how babies are capable of far more depth in responding to the songs and in the way they enthusiastically take up the intellectual life, providing they are wrapped in an atmosphere of affection and nurture.

The songs give guidance notes which raise the status of motherhood because they respect the observation skills mothers have and help them to build on what they see, sensitively and educatively. The songs set out carefully thought-through content with the baby's education at their heart.

This is an example of Froebel's concept of *freedom with guidance,* offered in a book for families to enjoy together. Although he felt that families, especially the mothers who were the main caregivers in his day, were keen to give the best to their babies, he also felt that they might not be aware and confident about how to take this forward in full, rich and deep ways. He was aware that women at that time were not as well educated as men in the main.

From boyhood he had been searching, at first unconsciously and gradually consciously for the interconnecting laws of the universe that he believed existed. The universe, the way people live together and become self-aware all came to be part of his concept of *Unity.* As explored in Chapter Two, the concept of *Unity* was a driving force in his explorations and learning. He wrote to his cousin:

> I am firmly convinced that all the phenomena of the child world, those which delight us as well as those which grieve us, depend upon fixed laws as definite as those of the cosmos, the planetary system, and the operations of nature; and it is therefore possible to discover and examine them. (Froebel letter VIII in Murray, 1929:11)

The things that 'grieve' adults led to his concern for the younger children during his time in Pestalozzi's school in 1808 and the difficulties they had focusing on what was asked of them. He later observed children of the families in the Keilhau community, and in his travels elsewhere, and become fascinated with early childhood play.

The importance of play in early childhood

Chapter Four explored how his interest in early childhood play deepened, becoming more tangible from about 1826 or so and coming to fruition with the invention of the Kindergarten in 1837. His journey in thinking about education during babyhood was an important next step. Froebel arrived at a point where he could take up his incubating thoughts which had simmered and finally came to fruition, but this was not until many years after the seeds of this thinking were there. Eventually he addressed his simmering thoughts about the education of babies in his publication *Mutter und Koselieder* in 1844. The publication, which took three years to prepare, presented illustrated notes for mothers followed by physical *Finger Plays* and movement songs. Konrad (2010:2) explains that Friedrich Unger, the former Keilhau pupil then teaching drawing at the school, illustrated the book. Robert Kohl composed the music and introduced Froebel to a lithographic printing shop in Offenbach. One volume contained the text and illustrations and the other the melodies.

The music and the movement

The music has been greatly criticized. Marjorie Ouvry a trained singer and Froebelian trained head teacher and trainer is clear that the range of notes is inappropriate for little children to sing. She compares the modern song 'Tommy Thumb' with Froebel's 'This Little Thumb':

> Both songs feature the baby's fingers, but Froebel's song is a much more advanced tune with far greater pitch ranges, from middle C to the F sharp more than an octave away! A child cannot sing that range but can internalise it and join in with 'What's this?' as the adult sings and draws attention to each of the fingers in turn. It has a new tune variation for each finger, is much longer and is generally much more complex. (Ouvry, 2012: 112)

She agrees with Colwyn Trevarthen that,

> The difficulty of the song is not the issue but rather that the child is in the company of a singer or a communicator and the relationship is the key factor. (Ouvry, 2012:112)

Froebel's vision was consistent in its vision to offer appropriate education at every point in life. Children cannot be kept still for long. He responded to the need for *self-activity* in the child, through *freedom with guidance*. He began to see that children needed freedom in movement and that lack of opportunity for this often led to what was seen by adults as naughtiness and bad behaviour (the behaviours which 'grieve' us). Building into the songs physical movement to aid the education of children was a powerful way of addressing the good tendencies of active and physical learning which is a natural and essential part of childhood and provided an infallible remedy to the human faults that come from the lack of it. The school in Keilhau and then the Kindergarten and then the *Mother Songs* gave physical movement a central place.

Perhaps because of his own childhood experiences and the strict upbringing he received with its harsh regime and punishments, he did what was consistent in his approach. He looked at the interconnectivity between children behaving as adults would like them to do, and why they might not oblige. He came to the view that in the case of babies, young children and those in middle childhood:

> Behind each human fault lies a good tendency which has been crushed, misunderstood or misled. Hence the infallible remedy for all human wickedness is first to bring to light this original good tendency and then to nourish, foster and train it. (Froebel, 1897:121)

Babies and toddlers need to move

It took longer, until 1844, for this thinking to reach the educational needs of babies. He observed bored babies, babies who were not spoken to, babies who were left to cry, babies wrapped up so that they could not easily move their limbs. Parents and families who wanted the best for their youngest, and who typically appreciated informed support in understanding a child's development, became a focus of his interest. During the time he was in Yverdun (1808), he began to realize that he had difficulty with Pestalozzi's belief that the youngest children, through the influence and love of both mother and father, acquire the foundations needed to prepare them for education. This began to impinge increasingly on Froebel's search for *Unity*. It is interesting to see how some thoughts that we have fade over time, but others become permanent even though the ideas are not yet clear in the beginning. These are thoughts which refuse to fade, and keep resurfacing, and sometimes take a more tangible form. It is often the case that when we disagree with someone, it is because they have touched on something which interrupts and disturbs our thinking. This was probably what happened when Froebel spent time and studied in Pestalozzi's school in Yverdun in 1808.

Partnership with parents

He was developing a vision of a whole life of education, from birth to death. Education therefore needs to begin from the moment a child was born. Although he was, like Pestalozzi, dedicated (especially through the loss of his mother as a baby) to the importance of family in early life, he felt that 'an education, even for the very young child not yet at school, needs skills which mothers and fathers do not "instinctively" possess' (Liebschner, [1992]2001:7). One of the teachers in the Yverdun school, Hermann Krusi, in cooperation with Pestalozzi, in 1800 wrote the *Mother Book* which saw early childhood education as a 'matter of the heart not the mind' (Liebschner [1992]2001:6). Here was a difficulty for Froebel, who had come to see human beings and their education as an interconnected whole. For Pestalozzi, the first step was for the parents in the home to provide a foundation from the heart on which to build a wholistic education. This provided what would be needed for the later education of the hand, the heart and the mind. By contrast, Froebel saw the physical body, emotional and social self and the intellectual life of the child as an inseparable whole throughout life. As he said:

> The manner in which we are educated, and in general treated, in our earliest childhood has, as we all know, a remarkable influence upon our emotions, our thoughts, our actions, during the whole of our life. (Froebel, letter IV in Murray, 1929:9)

The interconnectedness of the *Forms of Everyday life, Beauty* and *Knowledge*

While he was in Yverdun, Froebel began to ponder on his observations of the youngest children in the school, who were not yet 7 years of age and felt that they were struggling within Pestalozzi's approach. Although the object lessons provided children with tangible experiences, he felt they did not encourage children to make the thoughtful connections needed through what he came to describe as the *Forms* of *Everyday life, Beauty* and *Knowledge*. These were central to his concept of *Unity* and were essential if children were to make meaning that went beyond nourishing their senses, powers of observation and language. He had no wish to take away or replace the role of parents in the earliest years of childhood, but his thinking on the matter of early childhood education was incubating. It became sufficiently uncomfortable to cause him to leave Pestalozzi's school, although he did so with good relationships intact. He was always grateful to Pestalozzi for the ways in which the experience of being in his school for an extended time had helped him to begin to tease out his own approach to education as something integrated with life.

Incubation is not a sudden process (Bruce, 2011). His ideas about play and the Kindergarten were more easily made tangible because they could come alive through the development of the *Gifts* and *Occupations* in Burgdorf in 1928, which were in effect a kind of rehearsal for what became his invention of the Kindergarten in Blankenburg in 1837. The incubation of the *Mother Songs* took longer and did not emerge until 1844. He felt this constituted his most important work because the *Mother Songs* began with the baby's education:

> He desired to begin from the very beginning in a thorough manner. He is not a reformer of the art of teaching only, but of the entire theory of education. (Poesche in Murray, 1929:3)

The family was supported with the songs, rhymes, illustrations, music and guiding notes and so there was freedom for them in the way they interacted with their babies and toddlers, but with support and guidance. Froebel gave parents navigational tools.

The importance of observation: A scientific approach

Froebel did not rely on his own individual thinking in preparing the *Mother Songs* for use in homes and Kindergartens. He was very modern in this respect. He undertook market research and carried out pilot work before launching on a wider scale his *Gifts, Occupations, Movement Games* or the *Finger Plays*, rhymes, songs and dances. This is evident in his letters, in particular those to his cousin. In letter VIII he writes:

> A large majority of our games I have created, just as they are, simply by watching children at play, and then re-casting their games in the spirit of my whole system. Thus, quite lately, I have prepared a limping game, because I see boys are always limping and hopping. I have also taken your idea of a clucking hen, or hen-and-chicken, as the basis of a game which I will send you for trial. (Froebel letter VIII in Murray, 1929:12)

In letter IX he writes:

> To help the child to use his own body, his limbs, and his sensations, and to assist mothers and those who take the place of mothers to the consciousness of their duties towards the children and to a lofty conception of those duties, I have carefully preserved several little songs and games as they have occurred to me in the course of my life; and have given them the name of –
>
> *Little Nursery Songs (Koseliedchen) and Games*
>
> *to train the body, the limbs and the senses*
>
> *for quite little children.*

> I send this collection to you for your severe criticism. You, best of all, from the rich treasure of your experience as a mother, can pronounce whether I have or have not hit the mark at which I have aimed. Strike out ruthlessly all that seems to you unsuitable. And if you could give the little songs to mothers who have quite little children, so that they may test them thoroughly, or if you are able yourself thus to try them, I should be above all things delighted.(Froebel, letter IX in Murray, 1929:13–14).

A moral framework

He placed great value on continually reassessing his work, as part of a process of becoming. The *Mother Songs, and Games and Stories,* as discussed in the earlier part of this chapter, provide physical and active opportunities for learning. They bring freedom with guidance in the way active movement is encouraged, but not in a chaotic way. They involve language in meaningful ways. Froebel did not want children to experience what Baroness von Bulow is reported to have described as 'empty word teaching' (Smith, 1983:317).

Learning texts from the Bible was a typical activity in education, but Froebel did not wish to see this imposed on babies or in his Kindergartens. The rhymes in the *Mother Songs* are carefully crafted and chime with the illustrations to bring a moral framework which guides the family and educators in bringing up and educating children. There are nuanced and subtle, non-preachy messages throughout, which aim to cause thinking rather than endorse conformity to authority. The examples are of appreciating the work of people who bring things to the child's everyday life, such as the farmer who sows and cuts the wheat, the miller who makes the flour and the family baking the bread in the home. He shows people learning how to help with tasks, and why these need to be performed. Learning to take responsibility has a central place and does involve a feeling of duty but it also brings fulfilment – examples are of feeding the birds or watering the plants in the garden. The *Mother Songs and Games* bring the parent (and carers of other people's children) to Froebel's concept of *Unity* once again. It is always there, because interconnectivity is part of it. Through the *Finger Plays* and *Movement Games* children become self-aware, and relate themselves within their everyday community to others, and they are helped to see beyond to matters of the universe and how to make better lives and a better earth through their active efforts and involvement. Kant's sense of duty (Law, 2007), which brings fulfilment rather than happiness, chimes with Froebel's educational framework. Froebel's *Finger Plays*, songs and *Movement Games* deal with these issues in a sophisticated and complex way.

Liebschner describes in detail two of the *Mother Songs*, the charcoal burner and the dovecot. He suggests that the charcoal burner is 'a symbol of the importance of the seemingly insignificant' (Liebschner, [1992]2001:107). Respecting and valuing physical work matters:

> The hands are placed together, fingertips to fingertips, palm to palm and thumb to thumb, fingers straight. The wrists are now moved away from each other so that the palms separate while the fingertips also remain together so that a triangular shape is created. The two thumb-tips also remain together and with the base of the thumbs now apart, form a smaller triangle within the large triangle. Up to this point, it is a simple agility movement involving hands and wrists. The end product is in the shape of the charcoal burner's hut as in the picture. (Liebschner, [1992]2001:107)

In each song there are guidance notes for parents, grandparents or older siblings. It is important to emphasize that they are guidance and not instructions. Froebel encouraged older sisters in particular to help both in the home and Kindergarten using the *Finger Plays* and movement songs and dances. It would informally and powerfully equip young women for motherhood later on. This was another aspect of the emphasis on interconnectivity with which his educational approach is imbued. He writes about this to his cousin:

You will enable them, as future mothers, to educate themselves, and to learn how to play with their children, even the tiniest, in ways which are of deep significance, though at the same time perfectly simple. (Froebel letter IV in Murray, 1929:10)

As well as guidance notes for family or Kindergarten teachers, there are drawings which illustrate the verse. In the charcoal burner song, there are drawings that show a scene which a child living in a rural context at that time would find familiar (Figure 5.1). But it would not be so for a child of today. However, the key message here is in the way that Froebel demonstrates the significance of the scenes such that the sequence from making the charcoal, to its use by the blacksmith, who is then able to make the spoon that feeds the child, who sits enjoying the food on the mother's lap.

Froebel's *Forms of Everyday life, Beauty and Knowledge* are present here too. However, in this day and age, the song no longer passes the test in the application of the first *Form*. It does not relate to the *everyday life* of a child of today. This would be a reason for practitioners and families of today to say it has become obsolete and is not suitable for inclusion in a home or Kindergarten nowadays. Konrad points out that in 1844:

The circulation of the *Mutter und Koselieder* was enormous. We find translations in Belgium, France, England, North America, Japan, Korea and Russia. In the nineteenth century there were various re-workings and new editions continued to appear well into the twentieth century in Germany. (2010:6)

Froebel's idea would have been to show what would have been a familiar hut with the charcoal burning method being demonstrated in front and the two sons of the charcoal burner learning how to contribute to the family's work. Children of today do not see a blacksmith at work in a regular way. But they would have done in Froebel's time. There is a familiar activity of family eating in the third picture, but the clothes and kitchen itself are of another time. Liebschner points out that,

The details, encouraging conversation and explanation by the mother from which the child might learn, are simple, accurate and beautifully executed. Each drawing is complete in itself and yet linked by ideas to form a unified whole. ([1992]2001:109)

Froebel is teaching children to use their hands in the *Finger Plays*, to appreciate what they can do with their hands, and to value those who work with their hands. The moral messages are gently given, but they are present in a subtle and sophisticated form. Froebel hopes that parents, especially mothers, will have conversations about the pictures, but although he gives suggestions, they are only intended as possibilities. The third element of Froebel's

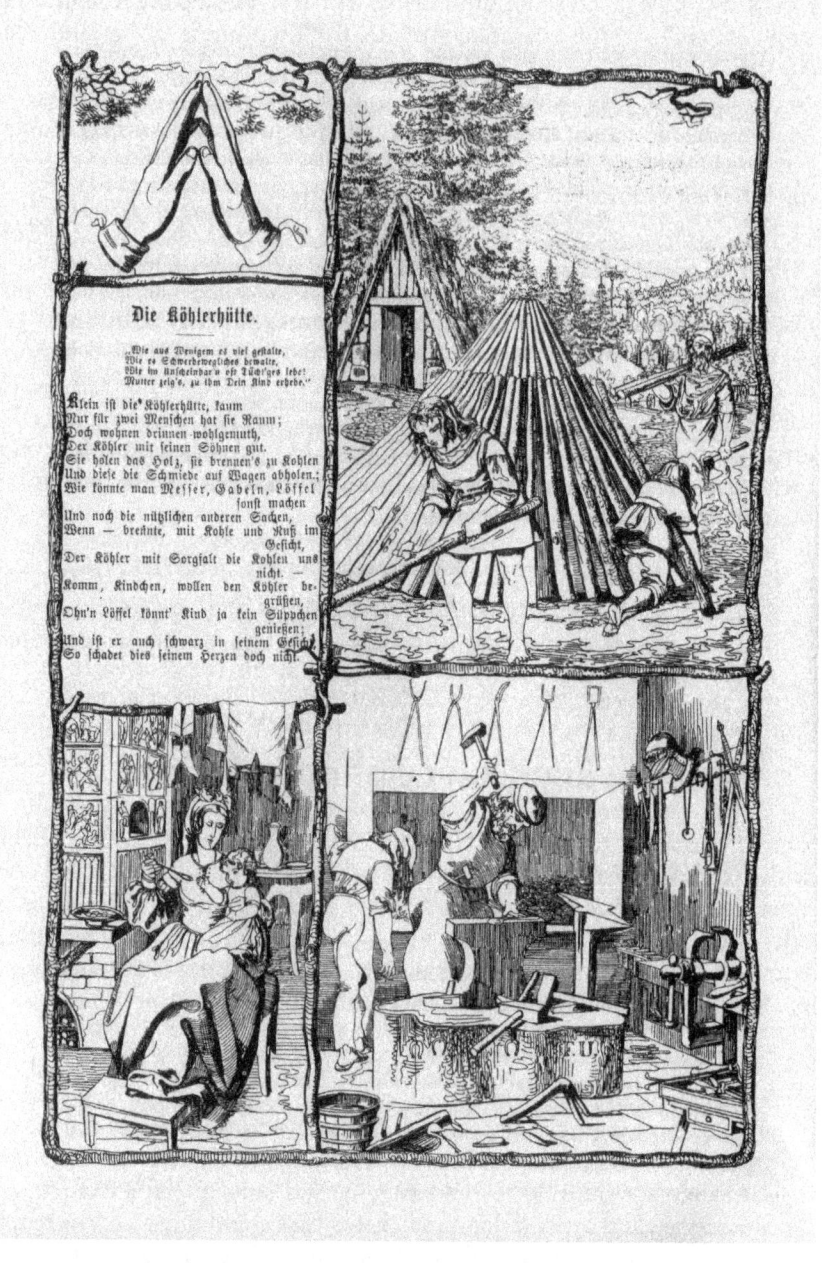

FIGURE 5.1 The charcoal burner, from the *Mother Songs*.

Forms, knowledge, does not offer discussion around the kind of knowledge to which children now can easily relate. Children might draw using charcoal, and they may have found bits of it if there has been a family outing or holiday with a camp fire, but the sequence of scientific knowledge that develops from making the charcoal to making the iron spoons and forks is not something a modern child can engage with. Using the hands to represent the hut is an example of *symbolic representation.*

The *everyday* familiarity of the scene is outmoded and the *Knowledge* is historic in relation to the charcoal burner and blacksmith, there is still *Beauty* in the inclusion of triangles and oblongs everywhere in the three illustrations as well as in the hand movements, but it is unlikely to grab the interest of a child of today despite the patterns, shapes and harmony of design. Liebschner goes into great detail with regard to the *Beauty.* This sophisticated element in the drawings is not included in later interpretations after Froebel's time. Liebschner ([1992]2001:112–15) describes the development of a trend, identifiable by 1905, to give children rhymes which keep them happy and which fill in time:

> Keep this book by you, and when the next wet day comes, the baby is crying because he has nothing to do, show him how to amuse himself; and if you don't know how, just open this book and see. (Stead, 1905:5)

The importance of relationships

The powerful recent research of Sacha Powell and Kathy Goouch working with research assistant Louie Werth indicates that the trend of using songs simply to lull babies into happiness or into sleep continues. Their research addresses the greater importance of singing in the lives of babies and very young toddlers, giving it the central place that it requires if the education is in any way to become Froebelian. According to them,

> 'closeness', 'stillness' and being 'in the moment' with a baby seemed to be rare events, with participants appearing anxious about being seen as inactive, not working. This project helped them to legitimise the practice of 'lulling' a baby other than when sleep was imminent. In this project, participants were able to hold singing and songs up for examination, considering and articulating the benefits that could often be 'read' in the faces of the babies in their films, with one participant commenting 'singing it helps them to thrive' (Participant interview). (Powell and Goouch, 2019:165)

They addressed the question: 'To what extent does singing further the managerialist agendas over and above more principled approaches to the education and care of babies, such as that advocated by Froebel or vice versa?' (Powell and Goouch, 2019:164). They found that,

> The project challenged participants to use songs and singing, vocalisations and motherese, to support the mutuality of engagement promoted by Froebel. Above all, the participants were helped through discursive opportunities, centred on pedagogical enquiry and reframing, to look at the babies, to notice expressions of emotion, to better understand 'interaction'. (Powell and Goouch, 2019:165)

Interaction is key to the Froebelian approach. As the research of Powell and Goouch shows, using songs with babies which hold meaning and are relevant to present-day families and practitioners is essential, but a challenge:

> While the Bee Gees may not have been quite what Froebel had in mind, he was not prescriptive in the use of his Mother Songs: 'those songs which arise or which come to mind on impulse of the moment, and amidst circumstances, are always the best.' (Froebel, 1891:62).(Powell and Goouch, 2019:164)

The emphasis Powell and Goouch place on observing and reacting to the way babies respond to and initiate with movement and babble when sung to and with is given strong support by Colwyn Trevarthen. He, with Stephen Malloch, has gathered together a vocabulary which chimes with Froebel's approach to the education of babies. The rhythmic patterns in the way mothers and babies engaged are variously described as musical or dance-like, proto-conversations, attunement, acts of meaning and this 'strong curiosity of humans was expressed in responsive smiles, calls and gestures which excited their mothers and "captured" them into the flow of the present moment of the exchange' (Malloch and Trevarthen 2009:1). There is an important connection here with Froebel's *Mutter und Koselieder.* They highlight the contribution of the poetic nature of the rhythmic patterns in these exchanges, and point out how this leads to cultural learning:

> We define musicality as expression of our human desire for cultural learning, our innate skill for moving, remembering and planning in sympathy with others that makes our appreciation and production of an endless variety of dramatic temporal narratives possible.(Malloch and Trevarthen (2009:2))

They go on to say:

> We believe education to be a collaborative task requiring intentional participation in actions, discoveries and feelings in the human time of shared movement. (Malloch and Trevarthen, 2009:8)

Reconnecting with Froebel's vision: The principles and practices together

Overall, it is the vision of what is the purpose and function of the educational possibilities which is important when revisiting Froebel's *Finger Plays* and action games. There is a moral framework through the concept of *Unity* which interconnects with the *Forms* and the related concept that education supports children in making the *outer inner* and the *inner outer*, and the *inner outer* and the *outer inner* in an iterative, self-driven and continual cycle. There is now an urgent need to develop something which is true to his vision which works in the context of today's world and once again makes family songs which spill over into group childcare and educational Kindergarten type settings. There has been a serious loss of Froebelian treasure here.

Reconnecting with key messages of physical interaction and relationships through making symbols together involving nature, objects and people, the *Finger Plays* the 'Charcoal burner' key has useful things to signal to us. There is a requirement for all three interconnected *Forms* (links to *Everyday life, Beauty and Knowledge*) to be present, and for adults spending time with babies to 'observe, support and extend' (Bruce, 1987:65) their initiations and responses to rhythmic and motherese situations that are in the moment. Being in the moment means creating a warm and nurturing atmosphere in which the baby can physically experience wholeness of ideas, thoughts, feelings and interactive relationships with adults who love them. It is useful to look at other songs to further explore these aspects. Cooking and meals are part of a baby's life, and in urban settings time in a garden or park, feeding the birds might also be an *everyday* experience. The weather when out of doors is another feature, and seeing a pond of fish might be another. There are *Finger Plays* about all of these. There remains the issue of their datedness, in the poetry, illustrations and tunes but it is worth looking at them in order to extract some illuminative messages of use for this day and age.

The *Finger Play* song 'Pat a Cake' presents the process of baking and eating bread and in a modern form is widely sung today. In *Mottoes and Commentaries of Friedrich Froebel's Mother Play* (1895a) Froebel explains how the mother, with baby facing her on her lap, holds the baby's hands palms together, with her hands gently at the base of the baby's hands. She then sings, clapping the baby's hands to show the patting of the cake. There are guidance notes for the adult showing the actions. The miller makes the flour. The mother makes the raw mixture in the kitchen of the home with the baby and takes it to the baker to turn it into a cake. Playing with babies in this way gives the poetry of language, music and movement in a meaningful way, in this case linked to food preparation and mealtimes. According to Froebel,

The influence of the word is yet more heightened by the law of movement (the rhythm) and by the singing tone (the mother's way of singing), because, in this way, the word has an influence on the mind, on the thought, by means of the feeling. (1899:52)

Contributing to making a better world

Powell and Goouch (2012–2015:26) in their research project explore the way in which Froebel creates a moral framework through the mother songs. They point out that in the *Mottoes and Commentaries*, Froebel links the child to the contribution of people beyond the immediate family in bringing food to the table, from the baby back to the baker, to the miller, to the farmer, but he also emphasizes the powerful force of nature. For Froebel this is God:

> The forces of Nature could not conspire together were it not for the all-wise and beneficent Power who incites and guides them to their predetermined ends. (Froebel, 1895a:126–7)

The forces of nature are too huge and intangible as concepts for babies to understand. However, Froebel believed that it was possible to take children from the real and direct experiences involved in everyday life to literal representations of life to increasingly more abstract, symbolic representations of life and deeper knowledge (Davies, 2003). The song about the weathervane illustrates this, making the *inner outer* and the *outer inner*. The baby can feel the wind as a force of nature and imitate the way it moves the weathervane through the *Finger Play*. There is great satisfaction in imitating the way the weathervane moves on top of the building. It would be interesting to know if Froebel chose to demonstrate the force of wind in nature using the cockerel on top of a church in the knowledge that Pope Gregory I had, in the sixth century, pronounced that it was a symbol of Christianity (Moss, 2019:57). The link with chickens continues as Froebel draws attention to the way the tails of the chickens ruffle in the wind. A girl's hanky and the boy's flag flutter in the wind. The clothes on the washing line are buffeted by the wind which speeds up the drying. In the distance the windmill sails rotate in the wind. In the notes to parents Froebel suggests making a paper vane to rotate as they run along with it in the wind. (There is a link here with his paperfolding *Occupation* explored in Chapter Six.) Froebel points out to parents in the notes that children will not as yet understand concepts such as air pressure, altered volume or changes in temperature that produce the wind, but they can relate to the physical feelings caused by the power of the wind.

In the *Mother Songs* introducing the charcoal burner and the weathervane there are different uses of the hand. Froebel believed that it was important to introduce songs with the whole body and limbs, then the whole hand, followed by the separate use of fingers. It is important before analysing the use of the hand and fingers to take a look at the way in which Froebel gives guidance to mothers in the use of the whole body, for example in the 'Kicking song':

> Your child is lying before you on a clean fresh mattress, in the strengthening bath of the air, after a bath of pure water has already strengthened him; he lies before you with a comfortable feeling of health throughout his whole body, and strikes out with his small arms as he kicks with his legs. He wants you to feel what he wants, to find some object by and through you and through which he can measure his strength and enjoy its growth; and what you read in your child's action as a necessity or wish, your fostering mother-love comes forward to meet. (Froebel, 1895b:129)

These notes are typical of Froebel in writing to parents or practitioners working in Kindergartens. He does not give direct instructions. He gives the people spending time with children status and respect by taking it for granted that they are good observers and carers of children and encourages them to simply build on what observation tells them, so that they do not impose Froebel's suggestions but carry them out thoughtfully according to their individual situation and with the particular character of the child they are with.

Creating the foundations for literacy

Jenny Spratt when head of the birth to seven services in an English local authority led the Early Years and Childcare Strategy. In 2007, she accepted the invitation for the Local Authority to participate in the Department for Education and Skills (DfES) National Pilot of Early Reading Development. The progress of the children was well above the national average (2007–9). The way of working with schools and care settings followed a Froebelian approach to the journey into reading, with a brief exploration of its connections with writing. The programme drew on Froebel's encouragement of children using their whole bodies, with limbs, hands and fingers, crossing the midline and transition from movement games on the spot to those involving travel from a fixed spot of sitting or standing (Bruce and Spratt, 2011).

The exercising of the limbs feature in many of the mother songs. Spratt (2012) became particularly interested in the importance of the hand. She looked at Emilie Poulson's work (1921) and current research (Khulman and Schweinhart, 1999; Mollenhauer, 1991; Goddard-Blythe, 2004) which chimes with Froebel's observations of the developing limbs, hand and fingers.

Both hands perform together, then one hand alone and then alternate hands. Once crawling begins, the hand is spread and closed more readily. The Pat a Cake song, examined earlier in the chapter, brings together the two hands performing the same action. The pigeon house uses the hands, but in a more complex way, and is performed by the adult with the child imitating if they feel so inclined. Liebschner (2001) gives a detailed description.

In the background a child is observing the mother as she sings the song (Figure 5.2). The guidance notes to the mother suggest that the left arm is vertical, and that hand is shaped like a cube. The birds can be made to fly out of their house by wiggling the fingers which are arranged on the top of the house, and become still once the pigeons have returned. Both hands are used to represent the pigeons flying. Hands can be swapped to exercise both hands and arms. A mother is taking her two children for a walk. The baby is looking at the pigeons on the path. The girls are watching a titmouse who has a nest in the hollow of the tree. It is typical of Froebel to have identifiable birds in the illustration, and a contrast to the phantasy birds pictured in most books of rhymes for children nowadays. The farmhouse belongs to the farmer working in the field. The dovecot is a feature. Children discussing together are walking down the lane, adding to the feeling of coming and going, with birds leaving and returning to the nest or dovecot. As a contrast to the birds, the mother and child next to the dovecot are still. This is, Liebschner suggests, an example of Froebel's *law of opposites* ([1992]2001:111). The notes to the mother encourage conversations about nature, including the identification of birds and their habitat.

The fingers are used in a more separate way in songs such as beckoning the chickens, beckoning the pigeons or the thumb in the a plum. Froebel introduces children to increasingly abstract ideas, first using the fingers literally, for example, with the thumb in the plum. The fingers are used to represent nature, people and things. They become nests, chickens, birds, the wind, farmers, buildings, baskets. Songs sitting on the mother's lap or sitting on a spot are important. But mobile children need to be able to move away from one spot. Songs and rhymes involving crossing the midline of the body are also important (Bruce and Spratt, 2011; Bruce and Dyke, 2017c; Dyke, n.d.).

The *Movement Games*

The *Movement Games* give such opportunities: 'Whenever I lead the games I always begin with the ball' (Froebel, Letter IV in Murray, 1929:11). In other words, the song refers to the first *Gift*. As always, there is interconnection between what went before and now. This is also the *law of opposites* because the ball was used quite differently with the baby from the way it is now used in a group *Movement Game*. For Froebel,

FIGURE 5.2 The use of two hands in the pigeon house, from the *Mother Songs*.

It is not at all needful to follow the order of the games as given in the series. This would quite destroy the fresh merry life which should animate the games. (Froebel, Letter IV in Murray, 1929:11)

The games give children some ideas, but they are free to build on them, interpret and change them to suit their inner thoughts. The recurring theme of *freedom with guidance* is here. Children who are just beginning to walk love to walk towards a person or fetch an object. This leads into the wander games, visiting games and representational games:

> Very rarely are the games mentioned in publications about Froebel, and several games devised by Froebel were never published … their study reveals a careful progression from the Wander games where the individual child is free to wander where he likes, and visit whom he likes, to games which involve two or three children, culminating in Circle Games where other children's wishes and demands have to be taken into consideration. (Liebschner, [1992]2001:128)

Yumiko Taoka has made a study of the Wander games (Taoka, 2019:114–22). The significance of walking lies in the way it combines whole body movements and encourages independence. In the *Mother Songs*, children in the illustrations are seen wandering and strolling to explore new things. In the Kindergarten and with older children this can be transformed into a game or a purposeful excursion, seeing things on the way. Liebschner ([1992]2001:98) points out that this turns into visiting and representational games, with a figure of eight leading to symbolic representation of the snail, the mill or the wheel. The games become increasingly social, from individual wandering to visiting others, and then representing aspects of everyday life as a group with greater exchange of ideas and discussion involving everyone, which echoes the community life. Christiane Konrad concludes that:

> The *Mutter und Koselieder* demand that we examine matters for ourselves; they do not offer any quick recipes for education. Froebel did not believe in quick solutions. Thinking coupled with observation are for him the focus of child education. Children have to put their own world together from their own experience. With the *Mutter und Koselieder*, Froebel did not intend to write practical tips for education but a book for family use, a book for joint activities involving parents and children. (2010:6).

Obsolescence

The obsolescence that is glaring in the content, style of illustration, words and music in the *Mother Songs* has led to a fading in their influence and use across time. Both Froebel's original songs and the later modified versions that followed were understandably discarded. New versions were created by Eleonore Heerwart, Susan Blow, Elizabeth Peabody, Annie Howe, Emily Lord (Prochner, 2017:7). It is, however, a serious loss for childhood and those who try to support the child's developing learning. Jolly or soothing songs, lulling to sleep songs or songs to fill a 10-minute gap in the schedule or amuse on a long journey are not educational in the way Froebel's songs were. The challenge is to create or find songs with poetry, music, pictures and actions which educate the whole child and cause parents, carers and teachers to reclaim what is important in Froebel's *Mother Songs* and *Movement Games*.

The *Mother Songs* constitute Froebel's last writings (1844). In a sense they bring together his whole philosophy and approach to education. It is interesting to note that they are the most neglected area of study by academics and researchers. This may be because they strike educators of today as too dated, too stuck in the historic era and cultural context of the time in which they were developed. There is another problem too. In Froebel's time people could read music as a normal part of their lives, whereas now they rely on digital forms of introducing music. Few educators can read music or play a musical instrument. A close look at the *Mother Songs* reveals that they are firmly located in the family context, but the *Finger Plays* travel across into the child's first ventures beyond the family and into the community in which they live through the *Movement Games*. Further examples are given in Chapter Seven arising from Froebel's observation of children at play. The *Movement Games* use the whole body and travel, as individuals and in a coordinated group. The content of the songs is of its time. There is emphasis on a rural life, with snails, fish, horses, birds, farming and nineteenth-century tools and machinery in evidence. The urban content is absent. Do the songs have any meaning for children and their families and educators today? With issues of climate change and moral bankruptcy this is an interesting question. Through physically participating in the *Finger Plays*, through sharing the book with family members, children begin to see in tangible form concepts such as kindness, taking responsibility or contributing to society. This is further developed in the *Movement Games*:

> The influence of the word is yet more heightened by the law of movement (the rhythm) and by the singing tone (the mother's way of singing) because in this way, the word has an influence on the mind, in the thought, by means of feeling. (Froebel, 1899:52)

The children

With a small group of children aged from 3 to 4 years old, the adult sang a song about a tree with green leaves. She held up her arms and bunched her fists to represent apples. The wind blows, and she sways. The apples fall, and she makes her fingers into a basket to gather the apples. One of the children knows the song well, and copies the actions, half singing and concentrating hard. But she has difficulty making her fingers into the basket. Several other children make the apples fall. The adult repeats the song several times, and each time more children make the actions. She shows the little girl how to make the basket. They sing this song, which the children enjoy, every day for several weeks, along with others that are better known by the children. Children join in the singing more and they do the actions more. It becomes more and more enjoyable to sing this together as everyone begins to know the words and actions and the feeling of power and belonging in performing this together.

The family songs, with actions, music, words, illustration of guidance notes (not instruction) for parents, bring together the different elements of Froebelian education. They connect with the concept of *Unity*. They illuminate *engagement with nature*. They bring alive the *symbolic life*, through the imagination and creativity of hands and fingers becoming characters as people, animals, plants, trees, machines. They involve others, as a *community* and they gently support children as they move from reflection on *real experiences* they had had, to representing those experiences in a literal way through using hands and fingers symbolically, to increasingly abstract representations of experiences.

CHAPTER SIX

Self-activity of the Child: The Gifts and Occupations

In this chapter the *Gifts* are introduced, and this is followed by reflections on their significance with some debate regarding their use, both during Froebel's life and in more recent times. The *Occupations* are then explained, with a discussion of the way in which they are now being reconnected with Froebel. Froebelian terminology is reviewed and questions are asked about the usefulness, or not, of the wooden block and experiences such as sewing, weaving, working with clay, woodwork, cookery and stick laying and more.

What are the Gifts?

Froebel developed a set of materials he labelled the *Gifts* and *Occupations* which arose from his observations of children. Observation was something he valued early on, as he was influenced in this respect by Pestalozzi, having spent time in his school in Yverdun in 1808. The *Gifts* and *Occupations* have been variously described by writers on Froebelian education. Sometimes they are separately described as a set of six boxed wooden blocks and differentiated from the *Occupations*. This is the option taken in this book, and the rationale for this will be explored in the chapter. Sometimes, the *Gifts* are classed as one set of apparatus and numbered from one to twenty. Brosterman (1997:40–89) cites an example of this approach. Whichever way the descriptions fall, there is an important and key message – they are interconnected.

The *Gifts* are comprised of a core set of spheres, cubes, cylinders and prisms. *Gift* one is a set of soft spheres (usually crocheted) which are the colours of the rainbow and which can be hung from a frame on a string or used separately without the frame. *Gift* two was in fact developed later than *Gifts* three, four, five and six. Froebel felt, having done a great deal of thinking about the Gifts, that this introduced the importance of the *laws of opposition*. There is a frame on which to hang a wooden, hard sphere, a wooden cylinder and a wooden cube. When these are spun on the detachable string at different angles, from the corner, the side or the middle, different shapes, such as prisms and cones or circles in the air, can be seen. Evelyn Lawrence, chair of the National Froebel Foundation points out that,

> Where the ball symbolised mobility, the cube was stable. And the cylinder combined the properties of both; it could be rolled or stood on its end. (1952:5)

The frames for *Gifts* one and two are made so that the soft rainbow coloured spheres, or the hard, wooden sphere, cylinder and cube can be returned to the box on which the objects are hung (Figure 6.1). There is a sliding lid, as there is with the *Gifts* three, four, five and six.

Gifts three, four, five and six are made up of boxes with sliding lids, each containing wooden blocks. The purpose of the sliding lid is that the box is introduced to the child by placing the box lid down on a flat surface, and gently sliding the lid out from underneath, revealing the cube made up from the blocks contained in the box. *Gift* three contains eight similarly sized cubes. *Gift* four contains eight similarly sized planks. In *Gift* five there are cubes cut in half diagonally to form two prisms, and some cubes are cut twice diagonally to form smaller prisms. *Gift* five chimes with *Gift* three,

FIGURE 6.1 The *Gifts*, from 1 to 6.

taking the cube and using it as a whole and breaking it into halves and quarters. *Gift* six explores the relationship between the whole planks in *Gift* four and what happens when the planks are divided.

The presentation of the box of blocks to the child has been described, but the putting away reveals equally important planning and thought on the part of Froebel in the design and use of the *Gifts*. Froebel encouraged children to engage in completion of their play with the blocks by arranging them in a cube on the lid and then placing the hollow box over the cube. Returning the blocks to the box and arriving at the cube shape demonstrates the mathematical relationships between the whole and the parts. The blocks are in a mathematical relationship within the box and with the hollow box. They are of the same proportions whichever box they are in. Froebel did not stipulate a specific size for the sets of *Gifts,* so this varies according to the manufacturer, but the blocks in the set are always of the same proportions. The *Gifts* represent the solid three-dimensional world of shapes, nature and the lives of people.

Positive and negative aspects of the *Gifts*

The *self-activity* of the child is of central importance in every aspect of Froebelian education. It is particularly easy to see issues surrounding the use of the *Gifts* and *Occupations* both in Froebel's time and in their use today.

Embedded in Chapter Five is Froebel's insistence that the *Mother Songs* and *Movement Games* should be used encouraging the child to make choices and to initiate as well as being offered the poetry, songs and dances by the adult. This is usually described as the importance of *freedom with guidance.* In this chapter the term *self-activity* of the child is added as another phrase from Froebel's terminology. The two go together very neatly. To offer songs, games and materials is not intended as a rigid prescription. It gives children a way of actively thinking their way into song making, dancing and poetry. In the same way, presenting children with a set of coloured soft spheres, wooden spheres, cylinders, cubes and prisms as wooden blocks opens up ideas paving the way for creativity and imagination to thrive. But this can only happen if adults encourage it and allow materials to be used in open-ended ways. Negative results occur when the use of materials is constrained by adults.

During Froebel's life, when he worked – with his invaluable colleagues, Middendorff, Langethal and Barop, and had the loyal and committed support of his first wife Wilhelme Hoffmeister until her death in 1837 and later, his second wife Louise Levin – it was possible to pilot and evaluate his educational ideas and to train Kindergarten teachers in the use of the *Gifts,* so that they could see in the Froebelian schools and Kindergartens what he intended in practice in the schools and Kindergartens he had founded.

This demonstrates the positive aspect of educators designing material for educational use with children. The importance of the *Forms (Everyday life, Beauty* and *Knowledge)* could be emphasized. Children's thinking is opened up to be creative and imaginative, using blockplay to construct symbolic representations drawing on their *everyday lives,* with furniture, people, fields of animals, houses, rainbows and so much more. The *Beauty* of their constructions is there to see in a very concrete way. There is symmetry, asymmetry and pattern. The mathematical *Knowledge* to be gained, almost by osmosis, is clear. The fascination and expertise Froebel acquired in the newly emerging chemistry of crystallography is evident in the design, which chimes with the Galina crystals described by Peter Rowland (Bruce 2011:116–18). The connections to other areas of knowledge also beam out, with *symbolic representation* through three-dimensional art, understanding of nature, storytelling and links to literature, poetry and singing rhymes. All of this is very positive. The early trainees in the Kindergarten movement were encouraged by Froebel to use the materials thoughtfully, understanding that this was not a rigidly applied method but a thought-provoking educational approach. It began with observation and tuning into children. Beginning where the learner is, not where they ought to be:

> He always maintained that his play activities, games and occupations would only escape thoughtless usage if the reasons behind each activity were fully understood. (Liebschner, [1992]2001:115)

Equally positive is the way that Froebel, throughout his life, was committed to the importance of remaining in a state of becoming. He ensured this process by his sustained and scientific use of observation followed through with what is now called market testing and piloting (Bruce, 2013). Having launched the *Gifts* in the light of trials with colleagues, family and friends who understood his ways of working, his observations led him to realize that those less trained in Froebelian education often offered the Gifts to the children in strictly prescribed ways, with no deviation in the light of the way a child responded or initiated. As his interest in the development of 'free-flow play' (Bruce, 1991; 2020; Bruce and Louis, 2019) developed he emphasized the need for the adult to offer the *Gifts* in a more open-ended way. In the school in Keilhau, working with children older than 7 years, Jane Read notes that Froebel encouraged children

> to observe their local environment, to make connections between themselves and what they observe, and to express themselves through activities of all kinds, including block play, drawing, painting, modelling, singing and stories, exploratory excursions and gardening.
>
> (Froebel in Read, 2017:136)

The importance of well-trained Froebelian teachers (Bruce, 2020; Bruce, Elfer and Powell, 2019) is threaded through the book and returned to in Chapter Eight. Froebelian education requires practitioners who are well trained, committed and well educated with highly developed interests feeding their intellectual lives, shared with children.

Negative developments in the use of the *Gifts*

By the turn of the twentieth century, fewer and fewer Froebelians had any direct contact with those who had worked with Froebel. According to Brosterman:

> Proficiency in the details of Froebel's technique, philosophy, and spiritual cosmology, which was hard enough to absorb under his tutelage, become that much more difficult after his death and the deaths of his proteges ... As later trainees were forced to learn from books, and from women who had themselves learned from books, important nuances of the original training were changed and abandoned. (1997:40)

Because practitioners were learning about Froebelian practice through reading and were trained by tutors who had not been close to the original practices, there arose the typical situation which follows educational pioneers. There was a literal implementation of practice. When this occurs, practice is at best pedestrian and at worst constrains and even prevents thinking, creativity and imagination. There is a switch from education in the real sense, to schooling, sometimes descending into mere instruction. Froebelian education spread worldwide (Read in Bruce, Elfer and Powell, 2019a; May, Nawrotzki and Prochner, 2017), but there was an urgent need to revise how it was practised.

The tension surrounding the way the *Gifts* are used and whether or not their use is Froebelian has been present in different parts of the world in the history of Froebelian education. Larry Prochner and Anna Kirova (2017:99–121) write about the way the teaching of Anna Bryan and Elizabeth Harrison in Dewey's Chicago school (1898–1904) led to a more open-ended than a conservative approach. Prochner and Kirova suggest that the *Gifts* serve as a 'gauge' (2017:101) in the illumination of this process. Kevin Brehony also writes about this period. He reports on the attack by Stanley Hall, who pioneered the child study movement and the introduction of laboratory schools in American universities,

> on the conservative Froebelians and their adherence to the gifts and occupations and the 'knights of the holy ghost' (Kant, Fichte and Hegel). (Brehony, 2017:22)

Susan Blow was one such conservative Froebelian and her response was robust. She felt that free play produced disorder and moral chaos in children (Shapiro, 1983:124). The first Froebelians who took his ideas to other countries had been trained by Froebel and his team. Subsequent Froebelians did not have this direct contact. The Froebelian movement Kindergartens spread rapidly, and the arguments about the best and proper use of the *Gifts* became a rallying call for what became opposing sides. In *Kindergarten Narratives on Froebelian Education: Transnational Investigation* (2017) edited by May, Nawrotzki and Prochner, different chapters are devoted to Kindergarten practices in different parts of the world. These include the Netherlands, New Zealand, Sweden, USA, UK and Japan. In every chapter there is discussion of the *Gifts*. For example, between 1898 and 1904 the Froebelian Van Calcar found that,

> The number of Froebel schools had grown, the principles were widely known and a good infant school almost certainly was a Froebel school. However, according to Van Calcar, then in her seventies, many of these schools were not worthy of the Froebel name because of a mechanical implementation of prescribed routines. (Bakker, 2017:43).

The revisionist Froebelians (Brehony, 2000) at the turn of the nineteenth century went about challenging the idea of what was deemed to be correct Froebelian practice, in the way in which children were required to use the *Gifts* and developed a principled approach to Froebelian education. It could be argued that in the way that it abandoned the *Gifts* and *Occupations* and instead began to embrace the findings of psychology, Froebelian education in the original sense, vanished (Nawrotzki, 2019). The *Forms*, for example, with the interactions and connectivity between the *Everyday life*, *Beauty* and *Knowledge* were buried. Froebel had advocated the enmeshing of all three, so that children made individual or collaborative constructions relating to their lives, which were patterned and symmetrical or asymmetrical, as well as leading them into knowledge of engineering, mathematics, and three-dimensional art with sculptures that were made of loose parts and free standing.

Evelyn Lawrence sees the first part of Froebel's book, *The Education of Man* (1826), as being full of wisdom and insight with a focus on education in the home. She commends this as extending education from home into school life. However, she writes:

> But another part of Froebel's doctrine, the detailed method of using the Gifts and Occupations, has been completely superseded ... so the stick-laying, paper-folding, cardboard-pricking, the pre-occupation with a few tiny bricks have all gone, and only the materials affording more creative scope, such as clay, sand and paints, have been retained. This is not to say that everything about Froebel's Gifts and Occupations was bad. Frank Lloyd Wright in his autobiography describes the delight he got from them

as a little boy, and it is perhaps not fanciful to see in the slabs and planes of the most impressive buildings in American architecture the influence, through him, of Froebel's tablets and Gift 5. (Lawrence, 1952:10)

This is something which Froebelians of today need to address, for many have been trained to discard what have come to be regarded as obsolete practices of the *Gifts* and *Occupations*, and instead to take the Froebelian principles and work with them. It is interesting to note the slight hesitation in Lawrence's final words in her statement when she reflects on the way the original *Gifts* influenced the architecture designed by Frank Lloyd Wright. Is it an either/or situation? Can both the modern wooden blocks and the original *Gifts* both be used?

The original Froebelian terminology has, until recently, been regarded as having little or no place in modern-day education, regarded as arcane. However, this book proposes a reconnectionist approach (Bruce, 2020; Bruce, Elfer and Powell, 2019; Bruce, Hakkarainen and Bredikyte, 2017). This is developing in the UK, South Africa, Kolkata and Western Australia:

It has begun to concern me during the last five years that a principled approach, disconnected from the original Froebelian framework of practices, means that in reality only half the Froebelian approach is being used or developed. This probably accounts for the reason why Froebelians are no longer as identifiable as they were, either those they work with, or even to themselves. I doubt that many practitioners nowadays stop to reflect, 'Is that Froebelian?' Even if they did, they would probably not know about the original practices, so would not be able to give much of an answer. I have come to the view that losing the tangible elements of Froebelianism has led to the loss of the principles having the capability of being navigational tools to any great extent. Froebelian practice has been mainstreamed more than Montessori or Steinerian practice has ever been. It was welcomed in the government-commissioned Hadow Report of 1933, and in the Plowden Report in 1967 (Central Advisory Council for Education). It was present in the *Curriculum Guidance for the Foundation Stage* (DfES and QCA, 2002), but the mainstreaming process, alongside the quarter of a century with a paucity of trained tutors and training in Froebelian education, has led to it becoming diluted to a state of near extinction. Bruce (2020:10)

Froebelian principles and practices: Reconnecting the two

There have been various attempts to revisit Froebelian blockplay. Patty Smith Hill designed blocks using planks, barrels and boards following an interest in Froebel's *Gifts*, but she was influenced to a greater extent by Dewey and Stanley Hall. She became a lecturer at Teachers' College, Columbia University, in 1905. Caroline Pratt was impressed by these blocks but created her own with proportions one to two to four. Community Playthings has a long tradition of making wooden blocks which chime with the original Froebel *Gifts*, and the influence of the Pratt blocks is also strong. Another example of a more open-ended approach is demonstrated by F. Guanella (1934), who wrote an inspirational article 'Blockbuilding Activities of Young Children'. Harriet Johnson who worked with Lucy Sprague Mitchell in the Town and Country School (1924) wrote an influential article 'The Art of Blockbuilding' in 1933. Wooden blocks could be provided in abundance, made by local carpenters. Children were often allowed to take a week working on their constructions. John Matthews (2003) suggests that this helps children to develop creative ideas in a more sustained way.

Nowadays the cost of sets of wooden blocks made from sustainable wood sources in the Froebelian tradition are such that schools and settings cannot so easily fund their provision. Consequently, their use has faded. Alongside this, Froebelians were no longer trained to understand their value or to see this as essential provision. Even if there may have been wooden blocks in the setting or school, these had often been relegated to a dusty cupboard, no longer used and with pieces missing from the set to use as a door stop. The increasingly high cost of wooden blocks has become a factor in recent times, but the lack of initial training of Froebelian teachers in schools and other settings has been another key issue. In the archival survey undertaken for the Froebel Trust by Valeria Scacchi (2019a:155) it becomes clear that practical work with Froebel's *Gifts* in the way that he advocated was no longer prominent on the National Froebel Union syllabus even as early as 1891. This was the examination taken by Froebel trained teachers.

In 1984, the 'National Association for the Education of Young Children' in the United States published *The Block Book* edited by Hirsch. In 1992 the Governing Body of the Froebel College funded a Blockplay Research Project directed by the author with researcher Pat Gura who worked collaboratively with five schools. This led to workshops and conferences, as well as articles and, in 1992, publication of the book, edited by Gura *Exploring Learning: Young Children and Blockplay* and a video directed by Bruce, *Building the Future* (1992). This is still used for training today in the UK. However, none of these overtly articulated a Froebelian stance except in passing, even if they were Froebelian in spirit and coming from that tradition. The domination of the principled approach of the revisionist Froebelians was strong. There is in practice connection to *Everyday life* experiences of children, together with awareness and interaction with the *Beauty* of patterns and symmetry, and the *Knowledge* that blockplay can bring about thinking that shows mathematics, engineering, technology, storytelling, visual art in three dimensions, and nature study as children learn about the trees such as beech and Californian maple from which the blocks are made.

Training helps understanding of key messages in the *Gifts*

The question is: Does it matter that there is a disconnection between principled practice and the articulated practice advocated by Froebel? There is a growing concern that it does. This is resulting in a new reconnection between the Froebelian principles and practices. In 2014 a pilot group was established (Bruce, 2020:269–81; Bruce, Elfer and Powell, 2019) to develop Froebel short courses and train Travelling Tutors endorsed by the Froebel Trust. What is both interesting and significant is the way in which progress in Froebelian practice is typically led by groups of practitioners working together, who draw on the expertise of researchers and academics in ways which chime for them. The Froebel Travelling Tutor short Froebel courses established in 2018 reconnect original Froebelian practices including the Froebelian vocabulary, the Froebelian *Gifts* in their original form, and take stock of the original *Occupations*. The aim is to reconnect the Froebelian principles to Froebelian practice, but in ways fit for the world of today. There is no wish to return to the rigid prescription of earlier times. In developing the courses there was a sustained dialogue between practitioners, managers and Froebelian academics who together teased out what the short Froebel courses should become following the pilot development work. This meant examining in depth whether the original Froebelian vocabulary is of use now. Practitioners in the thirteen Yellow Dot nurseries in Hampshire led by Jane Dyke with Paula Philips, found that this language was useful, which was unexpected. There has been a dominating tradition for over a century now that Froebel's *Gifts* and *Occupations* practices are obsolete and that only his principles should remain. Foucault's work

> stems from his conviction that the structures that organise the beliefs of a culture are historically conditioned. These 'epistimes', historical constructs, are determined by the social rules and practices that regulate discourse. (Law, 2007:34)

Is it true that there is arcaneness in Froebelian vocabulary? It is certainly the case that no one has dared to use it to any great extent for fear of being seen as advocating unsound and obsolete practices, and for failing to keep up to date with current research and theory. As a result of the pilot, terminology such as *freedom with guidance* and *the self-activity of the child* are now learnt by those attending the courses and typically seem to remain in their subsequent practice, because they are found to be useful. The trainee apprentice endorsed Froebel tutors, led by Dr Stella Louis, were equally enthusiastic about reconnecting with the Froebelian vocabulary. It makes such sense and can be expressed in shorthand phrases. This allows shared communication followed through with later discussion. It is invaluable for busy practitioners.

Froebelian language seems to help practitioners to both articulate and engage in identifiable Froebelian practice. It also helps reflection because it challenges current research and theory as well as being challenged by it in an interactive interrogation. Instead of academics and researchers instructing practitioners, there develops a healthier dialogue with practitioners leading their practice with autonomy and mutual respect on both sides.

The original *Gifts* are interesting for trainee Froebelian practitioners to study, but the more modern versions are in the main found to be of great use. Knowing about the original *Gifts* and using them while training is of central importance. The importance of the mathematical relationships between the blocks is key. So are the possibilities for creativity and imagination (Whinnett, forthcoming). The shapes cause practitioners to think about how they will present blocks, support and extend children in their learning. Practitioners find they are better able to critique sets of blocks which lack certain features. They understand the difference between plastic blocks, construction kits and free-standing wooden blocks and hollow blocks. Some children respond to the original *Gifts* with enthusiasm, and so it is felt that there is a place for both the original and more modern versions. Being able to articulate the function and purpose of the materials they use enables practitioners to offer the *Gifts* or wooden blockplay in ways which give the children greater freedom to be thoughtful, make connections and to be creative and imaginative. The need to observe how the children use the blocks is of fundamental importance. This gives children *freedom*. The need to show them the world they live in (Niemela, Reichstein, Sillanpaa, 2019), to talk about it with them, and to encourage them to illuminate this using the *Gifts* gives children *guidance*.

The example of Frank Lloyd Wright is important. He transformed the original *Gifts* into buildings with imagination, drawing on the Froebelian *Forms* in unconscious ways to do so. Children make a plethora of constructions with modern sets of blocks, as the Froebel Research Project found (Gura, 1992:200). The examples include trains, aeroplanes, spaceships, cars, rockets, see-saws, road, paths, caterpillars, elephants, fair wheel, snake, giraffe, fan-tailed pigeon, tree, star, flower, letters of the alphabet, computer, car wash, decoration, clocks, wheel-clamp, fish, birds and birds' nests.

What were the *Occupations*?

This is a very good question to ask in this day and age. The *Gifts*, in Froebel's vision of education, gave children experiences which could be put back together in the original presentation. The way the box of blocks was presented at the beginning was the same in appearance as the box of blocks when put away. There was a process of whole to parts to whole. There is completion. The *Occupations* are not completed in this way. Liebschner ([1992]2001:99) points out that Froebel wrote very little about them and suggests that perhaps this was to avoid rigid adherence to any textbook. He was certainly beginning to realize that unless practitioners understood the importance of *the self-activity* of the child and of *freedom with guidance* both of which held a central place, his vision could not be made real.

It is useful to look at the structuring of the *Occupations* to see if there is any buried treasure to be found. Before engaging with the *Occupations* themselves it is important to note that Froebel made a careful transition from the three-dimensional apparatus of the *Gifts* to the flat and two-dimensional, then the exploration of lines, and to the point, returning, with the *law of opposites* demonstrated with a contrast to the rigid wooden *Gifts*, to the hollow construction of the stick and peas to the soft and malleable three-dimensional clay (Figure 6.2). This could be made into a sphere, cube or cylinder, or many other things. Each *Occupation* connects with the others. He used squared paper to make a grid on which children could place the wooden blocks from the *Gifts*. This is almost never used in classrooms now, except perhaps, according to Liebschner ([1992]2001:100), by trainee architects, influenced by Frank Lloyd Wright. As Brosterman says:

FIGURE 6.2 Parquetry echoes the solid three-dimensional *Gifts* but in a flattened form.

When used to create 'two-dimensional' designs on the gridded field of
the kindergarten table, they became the "star, flower, and picture" forms
and the beginning of an aesthetic sensibility. The eye-catching, rotation-
ally symmetrical beauty designs even incorporated the idea of movement.
(1997:51)

Since Froebel's time there has been an industrial revolution in many parts
of the world. Colonial forms of education have emerged and have not yet
been eradicated everywhere. When Froebel designed the *Occupations*, he
was doing so in a rural, agricultural community. This is reflected in them all.
But does this make them obsolete? Helen May makes the point that

the metaphors of Froebelian kindergarten practice have endured through
time, adapted to their geographic relocations in place, co-opted later pedagogical trends and become inclusive of other cultural landscapes and
contexts.

(May, 2017:177)

It is the way in which the *Occupations* are used that renders them obsolete
or not. If children use the parquetry and are shown furniture incorporating
its patterns, they are being helped to learn history, about woodwork crafts,
developing fine physical skills, enjoying making patterns which are mathematical, artistic, noticing parquet flooring, fascinated by tessellations and so
much more. The key is the *self-activity* of the child combined with *freedom
with guidance*. The way this links with seeing and exploring connections and
thoughtfully getting to the bottom of things matters. This brings the *law of
opposites* and returning to the whole, the *Unity* through the *Forms*. Where
does the wood come from? Which trees and where do they grow? How did
the wood get to the classroom, and how have the colours been stained onto
the parquetry piece while keeping the grain of the wood visible? Does the
child want to make patterns with the parquetry using a frame, or does the child
prefer to use the pieces freely without? There is completion using the frame,
or perhaps the different shapes (diamonds, triangles, circles) can be placed
in different compartments of a beautiful box. There are possibilities for dif-
ferences in practice which open up the use of the parquetry in educationally
worthwhile ways. Relating the flat shapes of the parquetry to the three-
dimensional shapes of the *Gifts* helps the child to consider the three- and
two-dimensional worlds through the *law of opposites*.

In the same way, the *Occupations* which involve lines can be used flexibly
or in a rigid fashion. Conservative Froebelians like Susan Blow would have
argued robustly that there should be strict adherence to the rules. Froebelians
who were more flexible would have allowed free play followed by showing
children what to do, hoping to see them use what they have been shown as
a base from which to become creative. Possibly a closer connection with
Froebel's thinking and original practice, is to introduce stick laying, rings,

slats, jointed slats and interlacing but first of all to show children these in *everyday life*. Examples might be stopping leaves from blocking drains by having slatted covers, hinges, trellis in gardens, railings, railway lines, zebra crossings, venetian blinds, decorations for events, talking about the beauty, how things work, and opportunities to explore these materials in their own way. Children begin to explore lines which are rigid, whose shape cannot be changed. They then meet the *law of opposites*. Lines which are flexible and can change shape to wiggle and weave lead to learning about experiences such as sewing, weaving and basket making. With climate change a matter of such urgency, there is the serious matter of discussing whether to use plastic or natural materials. Materials can be updated through using wiring, to make electric circuits or garden wire which bends to keep plants upright in the wind. Children can experiment to see which materials are best to use for what, while learning to avoid single use plastic.

Drawing and painting are other *Occupations* which involve lines, but these are lines created by the child. There is a downside to this if adults turn the children's mark making into drills for vertical and horizontal and circular movement in order to prepare children for handwriting. This continues in settings today and chimes with the rigid conservative practices of some Froebelians at the turn of the twentieth century. Using a rich variety of pencils, charcoal, felt pens, chalks and paintbrushes of different thicknesses opens up a further range of exciting opportunities for children. It also connects with the pleasure young children take in making their own books, lists for shopping and choosing paper on which to draw or paint. Making paper is another *Occupation* which links them to industry as well as to traditional crafts. Printing is another *Occupation* which has developed and drawing in wet sand with a stick or a finger is another. These *Occupations* based around lines can expand very readily, so that finger painting comes into the educational setting. But knowing about the original Froebelian *Occupations* and the way they take the journey from three dimensions to lines, to points and back to different more transformable solids is useful for supporting teachers and early childhood practitioners to be creative and imaginative in the way they educate children and work with families.

Paper pricking takes children into the exploration of points. Froebel gave children the opportunity to make pictures and cards for celebrations by pricking paper that was placed on top of felt. This is rarely seen in UK schools and early childhood settings today. This is probably because of the impact of the conservative Froebelians who as part of their training made elaborate pieces which were remote from what Froebel had intended. The rejection of this over fiddly artwork for young children has become another of the ways in which Froebel's educational framework is seen as obsolete. However, when children have the opportunity, they take to it readily. Typically, they make patterns with their pricking rather than pictures which are more demanding to achieve. There is nothing so satisfying to a young child than stabbing at paper (or cardboard, play dough or clay)

Basic shapes

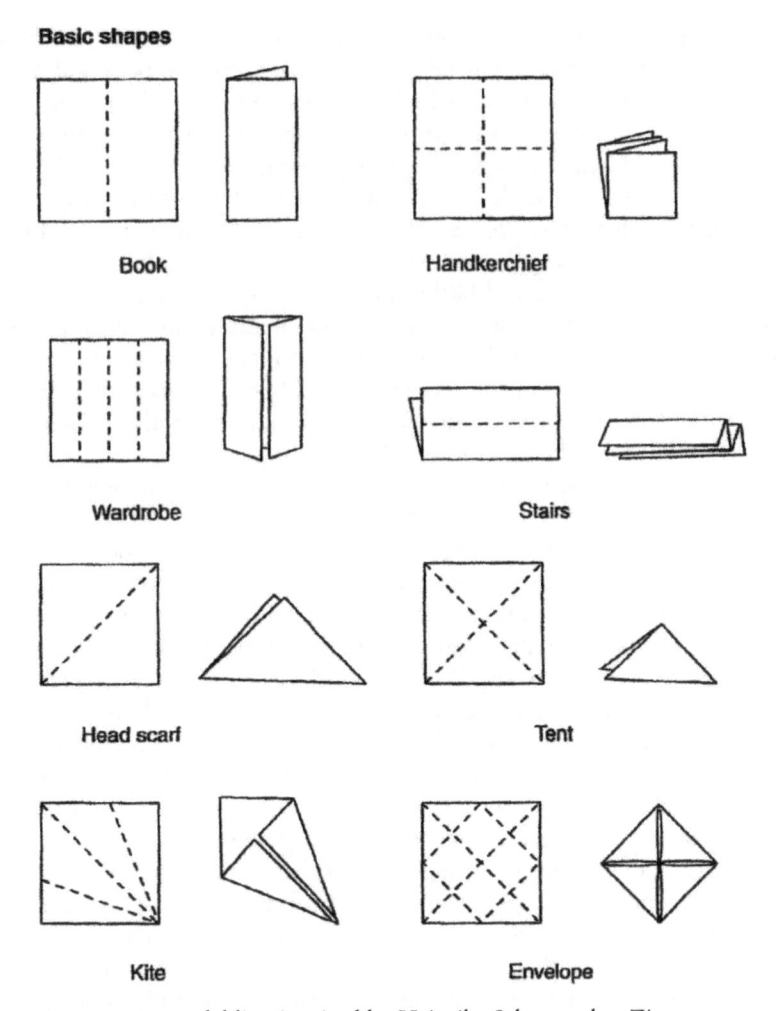

FIGURE 6.3 Paper folding inspired by Heinrike Schauwecker-Zimmer, (Source: International Froebel Society Conference, Jena, 2011).

(Figure 6.3). Paper weaving, paper folding and paper cutting have all suffered the same fate. Again, when children are introduced to these through the *Forms*, seeing aeroplanes fly, and learning how to make them so that they are designs which fly well, they become animated with enthusiasm. They enjoy making table settings by cutting, first fringing and then making shapes by cutting and folding. Making a set of doll's house furniture by paper folding is a very enjoyable experience for a child who wants to engage in it.

Weaving with yarn and thread or weaving with willow strips fascinates children who have been shown different materials and why they are good for keeping warm, such as knitting wool, making a scarf with woven threads or a fence using woven willow. Children will take trouble and make effort if making a mat for a doll, or a cover for a toy dog. Learning how to cut material as well as paper leads to making dolls clothes. Cutting and transforming various materials gives children a sense of power and autonomy, and this breeds creativity. Collage and the making of models results.

There are various kinds of construction kit nowadays, many of them made from the plastics which are devastating the planet. Whereas wooden blocks are free-standing, construction kits slot pieces together which are usually made of plastic but might be made of metal or wood. Froebel created the stick and pea construction kit. Either peas or clay could be used with pointed sticks to make very geometric constructions. The design on the cover of this book resonates with Froebel's stick-and-pea *Occupation*. The geodesic dome developed by Buckminister Fuller (1895–1983) is an example of the use of this medium. There is an issue of using food, so soft clay or Blu-Tack makes a good alternative. Learning about the importance of triangles in buttressing buildings and their strengthening properties can be consolidated if children are taken to see how buildings or football goal posts are formed. Exploring in the town, spending time in the garden, growing vegetables and joining in the tasks of everyday living such as cookery (McCormick, 2012; Denton and Parker, n.d.) and woodwork (Moorhouse, 2018) provide a wealth of opportunities for children to transform, through the *Occupations,* their everyday experiences. But children will take more thoughtful and engaged note of their *everyday experiences* if there is discussion with adults as they do so, and if they can be encouraged to be thoughtful about the reasons for things. This was something Froebel stressed. Chris McCormick gives the example of Fatimah, aged 3, who did not settle easily into the nursery school:

> Fatimah's chosen spot was close to the snack/baking table and it appeared that she was interested in observing food preparation activities. This gave us our first clue towards supporting and engaging with her. She began to come closer to an and then sit at the table. She began to respond to an adult's comment with eye contact and later a nod or shake of her head. She began to initiate communication by pointing, One day she accepted the offer of taking part and so began here engagement in nursery cooking experiences.

> It quickly became evident that Fatimah was skilled in a variety of food preparation related tasks. She ably handled all processes and became confident to reveal this. She became able to work co-operatively and to share her skills with others. Gradually language related to these activities was

developed. She then began to transfer her interest in food to other areas of learning. (McCormick:2012:138)

The *Occupations* give children opportunities to participate in what Lithuanian Kindergarten educators describe as 'folks art'. Froebel, in his thinking and designing of them, linked the *Occupations* with the world of work in rural life. They linked with the world of work as in Froebel's day. Brosterman (1997:40) is interesting here, arguing that post-Industrial Revolution the *Gifts* have less of a place in modern education. But he is placing together, as H. Poesche (in Murray 1929) does, the *Gifts* and *Occupations* under the heading *Gifts* (one to twenty).

Are the *Occupations* relevant in educating children today?

Is the teaching of weaving, sewing, clay modelling, drawing, use of construction kits, baking, woodwork, and so on obsolete in educational settings for young children today? The question needs to be asked: Do children need to learn to use clay with the possibility of making pots and artefacts? Is being able to sew or weave important? Does being able to build a den matter? Or is it useful to know about and engage in gardening flowers and vegetable and fruit, or to cook and undertake woodwork? With challenges to humanity on the scale of climate change, the importance of supporting children, families and policy makers in understanding and learning how to act in relation to the interconnectivity of the universe matters. Unless children learn about the connections central to life on this planet, they are uneducated in what matters for the future of the planet.

Reconnected Froebelian observations of children

Tom and his friend Sam were playing in Tom's home. They were both 7 years old. They played in the garden and decided to make a den. Tom had learnt some woodwork skills from helping his father at his woodwork bench. His mother was preparing lunch in the kitchen and agreed that they could use the saw and hammer, keeping the door to the garden open so that she could be on call. The boys spent the rest of the day making what became known as the A house. Tom remembered that to make it stand firmly it is good to have triangles. He managed to place a large piece of wood near the top which he and Sam could sit on. Sam operated as a helper to Tom's ideas, having no experience of woodwork. The boys then wanted to sleep the night on the top of the A house. It was agreed that they could. Tom's parents made a camp bed on the kitchen floor and slept with the door open.

The role of the adult is important here. This relates to *freedom with guidance*. Having rigid rules about what children are and are not allowed to do can often constrain creativity and curb skill development. The adult would not have allowed two children with little knowledge of woodwork and the nature of the structures of buildings to engage in this without closer supervision. But she could rely on one child having knowledge and staying near them, in case help was essential and needed or if they requested help. The *self-activity* of the boys enabled each to stay focused. One was trying to bring into tangible form his idea. The other was thrilled to be allowed to use woodwork materials and being helped to do that by his friend. The *Forms* were enmeshing as they do in the Froebelian framework. There was *everyday* observation encouraged and discussed with parents of how buildings stay up and how to use woodwork tools. The *Beauty* of the triangle was appreciated and seen to be functional. *Knowledge* of engineering, designing, planning was there, as well as measuring by eye, which meant estimating. This was practical mathematics. It also involved social knowledge. Tom understood that it is important his friend enjoyed the time, because it is more fun to learn together. His efforts to show his friend how to do things paid off. They could enjoy the result of efforts and sleep on the A house.

Mandisa is 4 years old. She was presented by her reception class teacher in an English primary school with Froebel's third and fifth *Gifts* having asked what was in the boxes. The adult avoided giving her the fifth and sixth *Gifts* together, knowing that this would result in a difficult clearing up session at the end as Mandisa was not experienced in using the *Gifts*. The adult showed her how to open them the correct way but did not ask her to have a go. She then left her to explore the blocks, staying near to unobtrusively observe. Mandisa picked out all the cubes and made an enclosure. Then she began to put layers on the enclosure and made walls. She used the prisms to make corner decorations, and the corners became towers. She placed them flat, giving up on keeping the cube formation with the quarter prisms. Then she disrupted the symmetry and rearranged the blocks to make one tall and fat turret on one corner, leaving a very small enclosure linked to it. She said it was a castle. She lives near the Tower of London. She loves the story of the twelve dancing princesses. The adults shows interest and asks if anyone lives in the castle. She replies that princesses do. The adult suggests she uses the small world dolls and the home-made dolls constructed from sticks, which she does. At clearing up time the adult comes to put away the blocks in *Gift* five. Mandisa is asked to have a go at using the technique with the simpler *Gift* three. It is clearly hard for her, and rather than spoil the pleasure she has had with a bad ending, the adult finishes the task for her while she watches.

At every stage be that stage. The adult needs to use observation knowledge. There is *freedom with guidance* but there is also encouragement for

Mandisa to stretch herself through *self-activity*. Quotations from Froebel are threaded through the book demonstrating how important this was in his educational vision. Causing children to think matters, but always in a nurturing environment so that it is not a frustrating, worrying or unpleasant experience. This only puts children off learning. Mandisa could use her *everyday life* experience of seeing a castle, yet it was also moving from literal to more abstract through her *Knowledge* of literature. She would, through a process of unavoidable osmosis, see the *Beauty* in her construction.

CHAPTER SEVEN

The Importance of Observation

In other chapters of this book, exploration of Froebel's approach to education reveals his consistent belief that human learning is a lifelong process. During childhood, when children attend Kindergarten and school, it matters that they spend time with adults who are trained to tune into their emerging thoughts. Education for Froebel was hugely about helping children to develop their thinking and ideas, but always as an integrated whole so that ideas, feelings, the physical self and relationships are part of each other. Children therefore need a nurturing environment, with people who understand how they feel and think, and need to be active physically in order to learn. He realized, spending time in Pestalozzi's school in Yverdun, that observation was a powerful way of getting to know children in order to help them learn:

> My teachers are the children themselves, with their purity and innocence, their unconsciousness, and their irresistible claims, and I follow them like a faithful, trustful scholar. (Froebel, in Murray, 1929:10)

Froebel believed that the future mind of the child is present in the play. This early learning is taken with us through our lives. Things happen as we move through life, but the bits of learning that don't get lost and which remain with us were there in our early childhood play. This is why he wrote, 'The plays of childhood are the germinal leaves of all later life.' (Froebel, 1887:55). Most parents (indeed most adults) do not notice the recurring themes in a child's play. It is so intangible. They might begin to notice more when the child's learning has some kind of product, unlike play which is all process. According to Froebel:

> To make the internal external and the external internal, to find the unity for both, this is the general external form in which man's destiny is

expressed. Therefore, every external object comes to man with the invitation to determine it nature and relationships. For this he has his senses, the organs that enable him to meet the invitation. (Froebel, 1887:41)

Froebel the scientist

Froebel's writings show his attention to observation. This was the scientist in him. Observation was how he built his field data. This enabled him to think about how babies learn, how toddlers learn and how older children learn. He could then try to match their thinking in appropriate ways through materials, games and nature study that he saw was important to their learning:

> To lead children early to think, this I consider the first and foremost object of child training. (Froebel, 1887:87)

He knew that in order to bring about depth of learning, it is necessary to engage children emotionally and to capture what interests them. He could see that this was a problem for the youngest children in Pestalozzi's school. He tackled these concerns through observation, as, ironically, Pestalozzi taught him to do. He observed the very youngest babies, toddlers and children to see what was important to them. This led him to understand the importance of play in learning, and he created the *Mother Songs, Movement Games, Gifts* and *Occupations*. All of these were in response to the data he had gathered through his observations.

He understood that children are thinking before they can speak. He observed hand eye mouth coordination in a baby as an object is explored:

> Therefore the child would know himself why he loves this thing: he would know all its properties, its innermost nature, that he may learn to understand himself in his attachment. For this reason the child examines the object on all sides; for this reason he tears and breaks it: for this reason he puts it in his mouth and bites it. (Froebel, 1887:73)

It is no accident that he came to realize that the sphere was attractive to babies and toddlers. The later work of the Froebelian Elinor Goldschmied (1910–2009) chimes with Froebel's observations. She developed the Treasure Basket (Hughes and Cousins, 2017:33–46) for sitting babies to reach for, to handle and mouth objects. Observations of babies using them reveal their fascinations. Different babies pick out different objects, according to their interests. As Froebel would suggest, the baby will know why they love an object, and would want to explore every aspect of it. Spheres are popular.

Empowering parents to become fascinated observers of their children

Froebel encouraged parents to be good observers of their babies. He was always very clear that working with other people's babies requires training. Instinct is not enough. Froebel said:

> It is needful that she should do it consciously as a conscious being acting on another being which is growing into consciousness and consciously leading towards the continuous development of the human being. (Froebel, 1887:64)

His observations of babies becoming toddlers reveal the excitement he observed that babies feel when they begin to walk:

> The smallest child who begins to exercise the power of walking loves to go from place to place. He likes to turn about and change the relationships in which he stands to different objects and in which they stand to him. ... Each little walk is a tour of discovery; each object is an America, a new world, which he either goes around to see if it is an island, or coast he follows to discover to see if it is a continent. (Froebel, 1897:243)

Observing the child who stays upright by tottering from chair to chair is now part of the established knowledge of child development. But what Froebel brings is a fusion of feelings with physical learning with intellectual delight, and the joy toddlers have in sharing their achievements with people they love and who love them. This might be called Romantic. Or it might be seen as understanding through observation the complexities of human learning. Froebel's noting of the way toddlers cling their way around a chair, returning to where they started, and realizing they have done that, quietly pleased with themselves (and repeating this to make sure) shows the depth of understanding of young children and how they learn. It is no wonder that he places great emphasis on the need for adults to spend time with other people's children to be highly trained. He wanted to support parents in their huge task of bringing up children and did not wish to undermine them in this. He wanted to support and illuminate the importance of parenthood. He was a great believer in the power of family love, having missed this in his own childhood. In the example in the following extract, he signals that later the child will come to understand what an island is when learning about nature and geography. Here are the germinal seeds of this knowledge in the toddler's play with a chair. In the same spirit the mathematics (lines and shapes) of later knowledge is present, and once again this is brought out in his observational notes:

> Here a child traces a table by its fingers along the edges and outlines, as far as he can reach them. Thus the child sketches the object on the object itself, as it were. This is the first, and, for the child, the safest step by which he first becomes aware of the outlines and forms of objects. (Froebel, 1887:77)

Another observation reveals the drawing (visual representations) children will be able to make later on. What is important here is that he is sees the potential of early play and how it holds the possibilities for learning that will follow:

> The faculty of drawing is, therefore, as much innate in the child, in man, as is the faculty of speech and demands its development and cultivation as imperatively as the latter. Experience shows this clearly in the child's love for drawing, in the child's instinctive desire for drawing. (Froebel, 1887:79)

It is fascinating to see how he realized that spoken language, although of great and crucial importance, is joined in holding a central place in education by the development and nurture of the *symbolic life* of the child. Drawing, as an example, heralds the beginnings of what will later become writing, mathematical, musical or dance notation and painting. The nurturing and providing for the development and cultivation of the *symbolic life* of the child is part of a sound education from the beginning. Just as he observed the exhilaration toddlers feel on taking their first steps, so he notes the joy very young children feel in drawing:

> In every activity and deed of man, yes, even in every activity of the smallest child, is expressed a relationship.(Froebel, 1896:237).

Chimings with future theories

It is not the aim of this book to prove that Froebel is supported by the theories or research findings that followed at later points in history which have been mainly carried out in the Western world. But there are some interesting chimings. L. Vygotsky (1978) sees future learning beginning with social relationships rather than with objects and so does Colwyn Trevarthen (2018). Froebel does give a high place to objects, but only in relation to relationships. This is why adults and siblings need to spend time and give love to babies, toddlers and young children. This is more than a Romantic position to take. Objects are attractive to children, but only educate children in the deepest sense when they are explored in the presence of people who love them. The Treasure Basket is a continuation of Froebel's belief that this matters.

Observations of babies and toddlers across the years would have influenced his creation of the *Finger Plays* in the *Mother Songs*. People matter, and relationships are intrinsic to the sharing of these between babies, young children and the whole family. The future power of play chimes with Jerome Bruner's thinking and his description of the way in which the child's 'incipient intention' leads the child to explore such that that any subject can be taught at any age in an intellectually honest way (Bruner, 1977:ix). Froebel's observations make the links between objects leading to the *Gifts* and *Occupations*, *Finger Plays* in the *Mother Songs* and later *Movement Games*:

> Who has not noticed how children love to turn themselves around a smooth tree or pole while clasping it with one hand and clinging to it with one arm. (Froebel, 1896:256)

This consistency in his observations of children becomes incorporated into the Mill *Movement Game*. He introduces the game, not to instruct children in how a mill works, but to cause them to think so that they take note and begin to make their own observations, to do their own thinking, They are supported in this by the Mill game:

> The object is to show plainly the spirit and aim of those plays. Their object is to lead the child to observation and apprehension and the life that surrounds him. (Froebel, 1897:256)

Because everything in the Froebelian approach to education connects, the *Forms (Everyday life, Beauty* and *Knowledge)* are clear to see. The knowledge here is to signal the workings of a mill, and to take part in a choreographed dance and to work collaboratively as a team. It cannot be overstressed that Froebel's vision of education developed out of his observations of children and a quest for what was important to them. Supporting children to become self-aware was key and is more than a process of meta-cognition because it connects them to the world they inhabit of people and nature, but also to the spiritual life expressed in the law of *Unity*. The interconnectivity of the Froebelian framework is present in his discussions with colleagues in his writings. He values the observations of others and does not simply depend on his own. But everything is linked to everything. Froebel says:

> A large majority of our games I have created, just as they are, simply by watching children at play, and then re-casting their games in the spirit of my whole system. Thus, quite lately, I have prepared a limping game, because I see my boys are always limping and hopping. I have also taken your idea of a clucking hen, or hen and chickens, as the basis of a game which I will send you by trial

I am also very grateful to you for the remarks of your dear little ones about rosebuds and green leaves. I shall make use of them in a game of flowers. We must have several such games for our summer walks, some to be played with real flowers, some as action games where the children impersonate various flowers and plants. (Froebel, Letter VIII in Murray, 1929:12)

Disagreements with future theories

In Froebel's view the educator needs to develop observational expertise rooted in the understanding and knowledge of how children develop, which becomes a resource from which the educator can draw. A definition of teaching is to 'observe, support and extend' (Bruce, 1987:65) the learning of children. Just as Froebelians have always come under critical fire for valuing play as contributing to the educational process, so the use of current child development knowledge as a resource is another area in which Froebelians have been and still are attacked. Postmodernists such as G. Dahlberg, P. Moss and A. Pence ([1999]2013) see child development as a series of norms and milestones based on Western understandings which result in normalized, standardized and culturally narrow views of childhood. They criticize the lack of emphasis on the contribution of culture to the ways in which children grow up and the importance of identity. These are valid and serious challenges to the way the Froebelian educational framework has always approached the resource of child development knowledge.

However, just as Froebelians have, until recently, neglected the cultural and identity aspects of child development knowledge and understanding, so postmodernists typically almost ignore the biological. Children, unless there is a disability or neglect, do develop binocular vision around two months, and they do sit before they become mobile. How they begin to do these things has cultural variations. Walking, talking and pretending develop in a cluster. There will be cultural variations in how these proceed or, in tragic cases of neglect, do not. Disability will have an impact. In the same way, children jump before they hop or skip and lose their first dentition around 4–7 years and so on. This happens all over the world in different cultures, with nature allowing wide windows for development and has been so since the beginning of humanity. These matters of the relationship and linkage between culture, identity and biology are important in assessing the possibility of being a Froebelian educator. Biology, culture and identity are part of observation:

The child, the boy, the man indeed, should know no other endeavour but to be at every stage of development wholly what this stage calls for. Then will each successive stage spring like a new shoot from a healthy bud; at each stage he will, with the same endeavour, again accomplish the requirements of this stage; for only the adequate development of man at each preceding stage can effect and bring about adequate development at each succeeding later stage. (Froebel, 1897:29)

There is no getting away from it. Froebel valued the earliest period in a child's life because, in his observations, it set the stage for later developments. But it is not a blueprint that is fixed in the way that the homeostasis of the Freudian framework is or as postmodernism suggests with fixed milestones and ages with stages. Froebel's own early childhood was far from ideal. What Froebel describes and has a vision of is an ideal education and an ideal life. He does not deal with deficit. He keeps on track moving towards the ideal. When things go wrong, he designs the Helba Plan. He won't give in to desperation. When things are difficult with delay in the building plans for the first women's training college or the Verbot closing Kindergartens, he trains Kindergarten teachers at Keilhau.

It is the case that, in his view, one stage does emerge from the previous stage in a child's integrated life and education, but his determination is to enhance biological development. He did not understand the enormity of cultural impact and how this affects identity. In this, he was of his time. The concept of *freedom with guidance* is useful here. The biological development of children will drive their possibilities to learn. The cultural context and the nurture they live in will influence the form their education takes and how their sense of identity is developed. If either of these, biological or cultural, are regarded in fixed or deficit ways education will suffer. It is significant that Froebelian education and its legacy from Froebel's original thinking is found in many parts of the world.

The entanglement of biology, culture and identity: Everything links

When biology and culture are viewed as interconnected, Froebel's vision of education becomes not only possible but rich in what it offers children, communities and beyond. This is exemplified in this description of current practice in a New Zealand Kindergarten:

Coincidentally, the flax-woven Maori *poi* has similar properties to Froebel's first gift, a knitted soft ball on a string. Chants, songs and dances from the various Pacifica cultures are also performed. The main cultural events for Dunedin Kindergarten are the annual Maori and Pacific Island Poly festival and *Puaka Matariki* signalled by the new planting season and was a time of family gathering, planning and reflection. Dor Dunedin Kindergarten children and their *whanau, Puaka Matariki* is an occasion of celebration, acknowledging the unique place they live in and giving respect to the land. The kindergarten as a cultural site is revealing of the coincidence of Froebelian traditions and current Dunedin Kindergarten practices that have shifted to incorporate indigenous values. (May, 2017:175)

A different cultural context is in a township Kindergarten in South Africa where the Asset Based Community Development (ABCD) approach (Kretzmann and McKnight, 1993) related to Appreciative Inquiry has chimed with the work of the Froebel Trust in South Africa. The school community value their traditional songs and dances, are able to speak several languages, but also need to be able to flourish in the South African education system which requires facility in English, both spoken and written. The *Gifts* and books in different African languages and English were introduced as the only costly materials. Everything else was on a low or no cost basis. This makes the practice sustainable and encourages use of traditional materials. It gives value to them. It values the singing and dancing, and the *Occupations* were introduced gradually, and with staff collaboration. Observations (Bruce, Louis and McCall, 2014) revealed that children responded to being active. Small groups rather than whole group activities worked best when using the *Gifts* or *Occupations*. Whole groups were ideal when singing, dancing and acting out stories. Small groups worked with clay (Parker, n.d.), stick laying, parquetry, sewing, bead threading, weaving, drawing with slates and chalks. This kept the costs low. Staff began to place sand, clay and water play outside on the shaded veranda as the mess had been a worry since children sleep on the classroom floors . The *Occupations* chimed with the traditional crafts and staff and children made these their own. A traditional garden with vegetables and trees holds an important place and adds supplies to the kitchen, with children helping in the gardening. The value placed on African traditions and their importance today as part of the process of decolonization are proving helpful through the Froebelian approach, and are used to cause thinking rather than to dictate method. The staff in the school decided to hold an open day and a wave of practitioners from other settings visited to see how the staff introduce materials without high cost, and to support the children in the way they used them. This led to a training day organized by the inspection team for the whole area, and the four workshops were led by the staff from the school. Biology and cultural influences (Read, 2018; Hoskins and Smedley, 2020) informed the observations.

A project in Kolkata funded by the Froebel Trust (2012–17) began with knowledge exchange between the team working in South Africa. The work was with street children and has taken root. This is another example of the cultural variation possibilities and the plasticity inherent in the Froebelian approach to education. The children attending the Parivar Settings were of a wide age range, and attendance varied. Staff in the school began to find that having the *Gifts* and *Occupations,* and Indian songs that chimed with the Froebelian *Finger Plays* from *Mother Songs* and action songs from the *Movement Games* raised the interest of the children. Behaviour was calmer and children focussed on what they were doing and responded with enjoyment to being given choices. Staff observed older children understanding mathematical concepts and numbers through the practical activities. They enjoyed drawing and began writing on their drawings. Engagement with nature was a challenge. The following are teacher reports given at a conference organized by the Froebel Trust so that staff in the different settings could exchange ideas and observations:

The classroom used to be disrupted because of poor behaviour; not now as the children are keen to learn and show their own interests ... Salu, 5 years, is paralysed on one side of his body. When he started school he cried all the time. The teacher gave him paper and pens to draw and he has learnt to draw straight lines and making letter shapes. He also likes to play with the blocks. He has made friends and looks forward to coming to school.

Sabana observes the children and their play and asks questions to make a story. She has started to introduce planting, but it is difficult to maintain over the weekend period; she asked the police to water the plants, but they were too busy. She uses clay but things dry out very quickly. We talked about how dry clay can be reconstituted with water ... Roudiel, 7 years, has never been to school before. He showed interest in sewing and came to learn about numbers and counting through sewing. He arrives early every day. (Holroyd, 2014:8–9; Holroyd et al., 2019:110–11)

Observation is of central importance, as the examples of Froebelian Kindergartens in different parts of the world show. The Glory School in Japan (Nishida, 2019:53–6) is an example of a Kindergarten that is culturally Japanese, although founded by an American Christian missionary in the early nineteenth century, still flourishing with its long established Froebelian tradition:

The kindergarten and training school she created has become a model for early childhood education in Japan. Howe's work has not ended and the spirit of what she implemented, her influence and the philosophy and practice of Froebel lives on among her followers in Japan. Every March, for the Japanese Dolls Festival the Glory Kindergarten invites children from international kindergartens in Kobe, such as Kobe Chinese Kindergarten, the Deutsche School Kobe, Kobe European Kindergarten and Canadian Academy Kindergarten. All the children play, sing and dance together for fun. It is considered to be international education and peace education as Howe implemented a century ago, which helps children develop the

attitude and behaviours to live inharmony with people who have different values, backgrounds and beliefs. (Nishida, 2014:7)

The concept of *Unity* is present here in ways that are suited to the Japanese
context. This is the case in all the examples given. Understanding the self in
relation to others and the world of people, nature and universe is of central
importance in Froebelian education. In Chapter Eight attention is paid to
the way that teachers and other Froebelian educators are trained so that
understanding of both biological and cultural dimensions of observation
are embedded in the concept of *Unity*. This relies on observation being a
valued tool in getting to know the child, the community and how these are
interconnected with the wider world.

Froebel understood that making the world a better place begins with the
child, but it involves adults engaging with children and tuning into what
fascinates them. Then it is possible to share with them what is known, and
to explore new knowledge with them. None of this is possible unless observation is built into the ways of working with children. According to Read,

> Froebel's kindergarten pedagogy has travelled across the globe, taking
> on elements of local culture and practice as well as responding to the
> welter of new ideas and theories from different disciplines. Rather than
> becoming an increasingly outdated pedagogy, this ability to incorporate
> new conceptions about young children's growth and development while
> remaining true to core Froebelian principles has ensured its continuing
> relevance for teachers and practitioners into the twenty-first century.
> (Read, 2019a:18, in Bruce, Elfer and Powell)

The way in which the principles have ensured continuing relevance is in
the way they support practitioners to be sufficiently flexible and sensitive
to both the cultural context and the development biologically of the child
in the way that they work with the basics of *Gifts, Occupations, Mother
Songs, Movement Games,* play and *Engagement with Nature.* Jane Whinnett
(2006:58–79) emphasizes the use of observation in achieving this. She uses
both anecdotal observations (remembered after the event) and narrative
observations (noted at the time). During the course of a year Ross (3 years at
the beginning) spends time playing with water flow, tubes being connected
and watching bubbles, making fountains and being fascinated making water
leaks from tubes. Over the year she notes:

> I experienced the wholeness of his learning both in part of the planning
> and reflecting on the documentation when he moved on to school. For
> me the unity comes from the conceptual coherence in the experiences we
> offered, the level of involvement in those experiences and the relevance of
> the experiences to the child's intentions. (Whinnett, 2006:76)

How observation informs planning

The planning was possible because of the observations. Stella Brown writes about the seasons as a natural planning model in the Froebelian nursery school under her headship:

> The flexible cadence of the natural work provides us with a perfect pace and rhythm for observation, investigation, exploration and reflection in a most meaningful context where children experience ownership, responsibility and autonomy for their space and place (Brown, 2012:38).

> Summer: Angela was very excited to discover the live caterpillars in a pot in the nursery. She asked lots of questions and used a fact book with an adult to find information. She watched very closely on the first day and told other children about her discovery. At home time she took her mum to look at the caterpillars and retold factual information that she had learned that day through sensitive interaction with an adult. Her interest was consistent. Each day she observed and talked about change and size. Other children were interested but Angela began to take ownership of the caterpillars. When she arrived one day to find chrysalis in the pot instead of caterpillars she was fascinated. She became familiar with the theory of the stages in the life cycle but the first -hand, real-life experience was profound. (Brown, 2012:33)

Just as Froebel had acted on his observations of children in planning the curriculum, so have the Froebelians who have followed his guidance. Observations matter. Nowadays they allow Froebelians to carefully document a child's progress over time and show how the adults have planned experiences which 'observe, support and extend' (Bruce, 1987:65) the child's learning. It has become possible to make digital records (Flewitt and Cowan, 2020) with photographs and films and annotations. Families enjoy viewing these, and they also give powerful observations and documentation of children's learning and the way adults have planned to help them learn both as individuals and as a group.

Other published examples of documentation arising from observation in the Froebelian tradition include: Susan Isaacs in the Malting House School (1930; 1933); Athey (1990) in the Froebel Research Nursery in the Froebel College (1972–7); Bruce, Gura and the collaborative team of five schools observing and exploring blockplay based in the Froebel College, Roehampton (Gura , 1992); Bartholomew and Bruce (1994) in the Redford House Workplace Nursery in the University of Roehampton and Queen Mary Hospital (1994); the Craigmillar Cluster, Edinburgh (Bruce, 2004); South Africa (Bruce, Louis and McCall, 2014). All of these publications are still used in practice. The kind of research which moves practice forward takes place when observation and documentation are combined with discussion, knowledge exchange and analysis. This resonates with the way the staff worked together in Keilhau and Blankenburg.

Observation in the Froebelian tradition is about knowing where children are in their learning. Marjatta Kalliala trained at the Helsinki Kindergarten college. She identifies three ways to work out the adult role in observing children's play. There must be sensitivity to play, informed observation of it and the adult needs to know the world of the children:

> Educators who do not really 'see' the child, cannot fully bear their pedagogical responsibility … be externally passive and internally active was one of the vital Froebelian slogans that directs the conscious observation of children. The adult did not actively participate in play, but instead observed consciously what the playing is like. (Kalliala, 2006:124)

The children

Two children 3 and 5 years old, had been to a show at a children's theatre which involved mermaids. They put an old sheet over the table and crept inside. It was the theatre. They used paper dolls cut out by an adult, stretched out to be the audience. They shone a torch on a box (able to do so after asking their father to change the battery) that became the stage. They used home-made stick dolls (made together with their Aunt Hannah on a previous occasion) to capture parts of the story, but all of a moment, they wanted to put on the mermaids outfits their aunt had made out of strips of material tied at the bottom. They could walk inside these costumes in a wiggly way. They rested in the sea cave (under the table) with the paper dolls becoming sea fairies. They fetch shells they had previously collected at the beach on holiday from their bedroom and put them into the cave. They tore newspaper and made it seaweed.

They are using *everyday life experience,* but it is moving from a literal 'take' to more abstract *symbolic life.* They have been to the theatre, spent time on beaches and in the sea. They use their previous *engagement in nature* with the sea shells and sea weed. They know about real fish and like the idea of mermaids. They have grasped the idea that you when pretend you can rearrange reality *symbolically.* There is *self-activity.* The role of the adult is not dominating, but adults are there. They help with props in a backstage way. They are quietly observing and encouraging deeper play in the way that the Finnish Froebelian, Marjatta Kalliala, was taught to actively observe in her training.

The *Gifts, Occupations, Mother Songs* and *Movement Games* as well as the experiences given to children in the garden and landscapes beyond all emerged from Froebel's observations. The same applies to his deep respect and understanding of the value of play. His scientific training led in this and enabled him to share this educational approach with parents and those he trained as teachers.

CHAPTER EIGHT

The Importance of Family and Community, Highly Trained, Mature and Educated Teachers and Practitioners

The family

There is a recurring theme in Froebel's framework which demonstrates a deep valuing of the family and the need for children to be educated so that they are committed to making a positive contribution to and participation in their community and society at large. Froebel's wistful yearning for the love and nurturing that children need to receive in families is evident. He does not articulate the impact of dysfunctional family life, perhaps because of his painful experiences in his own life. In this respect, the criticism which can be levelled at him, that he holds an idealistic view of family life, is inarguable

Perhaps a more realistic part of his thinking lies in his view that parents, especially mothers, should not be left alone and unsupported in bringing up their children. This chimes with the African saying that it takes a village to bring up a child. He recognizes how exhausting and overwhelming it is to be a parent. The emotional involvement results at times in what A. Damasio (2004) describes as raw emotions. The Baroness von Marenholtz-Bulow (1810–1893), who trained in Keilhau was a great supporter of Froebel, reports that Froebel said:

As educators of mankind, the women of the present time have the highest duty to perform, while hitherto they have been scarcely more than the *beloved* mothers of human beings. (Von Marenholtz-Bulow, 1891:179, emphasis in the original)

Families are no longer seen as a standard entity. Instead, they are understood to be varied and diverse. Patterns of family organization and structure differ in different parts of the world but also within communities, countries and under different circumstances. The situations in which refugee families find themselves has become a major issue in war-torn parts of the world, and where families flee persecution and violence (El Gemayel, 2020). No two families are the same, and no two families live in exactly the same way.

Despite the narrower world which Froebel inhabited, compared with the world of today, and the views of the roles of the fathers and mothers that he held, intuitively he does seem to recognize the uniqueness of each family. He felt that it was too daunting a task for parents to be left alone and unsupported in bringing up their children, isolated from their community. There are many parents bringing up their children in a community. Froebel is not referring to *a community*. He is concerned with parents feeling part of *their community*. A sense of belonging matters in Froebel's thinking. It is interesting that Froebel chose to found his school in a rural community, in a small village, where everyone knew everyone and there was interconnectivity in the way they worked together and were neighbours. He wanted the school to be at the heart of this community.

Empowering parents

Parents, in Froebel's view, need encouragement and support. They need to be empowered. This is very different from telling parents how to bring up their children. There are two key elements in Froebel's approach to empowering parenthood. The first is that trained Froebelians should respect parents and the families they work with. (Bruce, 2015; Bruce, 1987; Athey, 1990). For him,

Today the most urgent need in education is that the school should be united with the life of home and family. (Froebel, in Lilley, 1967:156)

However, there is contrasting interpretation of what it means to be a Froebelian educator which is less inclusive. Nelleke Bakker examines the way in which Elise Van Calcar (1822–1904) in the Netherlands trained what she described as 'civilized' young women in the science of motherhood. This is an interesting example of centration on aspects of Froebel's thinking and interpreting them according to her own inclinations. In this way, there developed deviations from his central messages.

Parenting can be a lonely and anxious endeavour unless there is a supportive community which the family is part of. With parents working outside the home in many countries today, often living far from their extended family in a nuclear mode, single parenthood and same sex parenting there are challenges. Early childhood group care settings might be able to give some support, but this depends to a great degree on government funding. For refugee families (El Gemeyal, 2020), the loss of the extended family and community is devastating. The Froebelian approach sees schools and early childhood settings as part of the community, together with parents and children. But settings and schools need to build the relationships with and between parents that bring a sense of belonging and feeling supported. The school in Keilhau (founded in 1817) and the Kindergarten in Blankenburg (founded in 1837) demonstrate this. There are opposing approaches to working with parents. One is a deficit mode, which Froebelians reject. Building on strengths and empowering parents is embraced by Froebelians (Bruce, 1987; 2020).

For Froebel, the mother who spends time with her children is a key person in their early education, but he also includes fathers, siblings and grandparents. Froebel's emphasis on the role of the mother was influenced by two things. One was, as discussed in earlier chapters of this book, his yearning for his mother and the pain he felt at her loss in his early childhood. The other was his belief that motherhood should be given a higher status, because it was the foundation of the child's development. He saw education as a from birth to the end of life process and so early nurturing and support were important in bringing about the flourishing of children from birth in their learning, so that they think for themselves, have ideas, understand themselves and how they are part of the community, the world of people and the universe of nature. The nurturing of children's interests is one strand which brings, in very meaningful ways, a rich intellectual life, full of satisfaction, energizing and harnessing the natural motivation that is intrinsic in babies and toddlers and protecting this from damage as children grow up. But as well as fulfilling the needs of the emerging strong self, Froebel also reminds us that children are interconnected with their families and, through them, to the communities and the wider world.

Froebel is clear that parents do not need to be told what to do. But they appreciate professionals who know about child development, and who use this to support them by articulating what they intuitively know. As he says in his letter:

You will enable them, as future mothers, to educate themselves, and to learn how to play with their children, even the tiniest, in ways which are of deep significance, though at the same time perfectly simple. (Froebel letter IV in Murray, 1929:10)

Observation matters

An example of working in the Froebelian tradition during the 1970s was the way in which Chris Athey made partnerships with parents in the Froebel Nursery Research School, and her thinking and way of working in the Froebelian tradition was a role model for the author of this book. She says:

> Nothing gets under the parent's skin more quickly and more permanently than the illumination of his or her own child's behaviour. The effect of participation can be profound. (Athey, 1990:66)

A parent's intuition does not need words. But professionals working with other people's children do need to be articulate and to share the knowledge they have. Observation, child development, curriculum, pedagogy and subject knowledge are all necessary and important parts of the expertise of professional practitioners. Froebel was consistent in his way of working with parents. He observed first and helped parents to join in, gather thoughts and ways forward and to pool in partnership what they saw the children do, and how they were learning.

Froebel's attitude to the role of women

Just as Froebel was both conventional and individualistic, but always inclusive in his approach to his religion, so it was with his work with parents and families. On the one hand, he had a very progressive view of the intellectual capabilities of women. He put enormous energy into campaigning to give them greater access to education. He founded (1849) what was possibly the first Kindergarten training college for women to become teachers. He believed that women would make ideal teachers of young children. Very few were sufficiently educated at this time to be knowledgeable enough to teach older children, but he realized that a start could be made by creating a Kindergarten training school for women. Caroline Holzhausen had influenced his belief in women having intellectual potential, when he was a tutor to her sons. However, although these thoughts were revolutionary in the 1840s, Froebel was conventional in regarding the place of women being to work with children. In the *Mother Songs* publication there is an illustration of the mother with a boy and a girl. The girl stands on a sphere and the boy on a cube. The former depicts harmony, and the latter a solid foundation. Froebel gives different roles to women and men, but he wants to raise the status of women and to expand the contribution they are able to make, but it is still within their traditional role.

His breadth of vision did not expand as far as seeing the possibilities of women becoming engineers or prime ministers. But it was a groundbreaking start in that direction. Almost two hundred years on there is not yet equality between men and women in many respects, at home or in the workplace in many parts of the world, including Western countries. Women, in his thinking, were to remain the nurturers of little children but could also become highly professional educators as trained and qualified teachers, to develop their intellectual lives as well as that of their children. This opened the opportunity for women to work beyond their family circle and to move into contributing in a deeper way to their community, working with other people's children and not simply within their own family context. It is important to remember that at this time only men were regarded as fit to train as teachers of young or older children.

Developing a community of Froebelian practice

Froebel seems to have chosen Keilhau as the place to locate his school in 1817 after considerable research. He decided on a remote rural, very small agricultural village with only about twenty houses and a church which was very traditional. He was almost certainly influenced by the idealist philosophers and scientists such as Christian Samuel Weiss and thinkers such as Jean-Jacques Rousseau and Joann Wolfgang von Goethe together with the Romantic view that permeated, which led him to seek a unifying principle:

> Being at one with nature, of finding divinity in nature, and of character and understanding being developed by returning to a simple life in rural surroundings. (Smith, 1983:306)

He felt he would be less obvious and open to public scrutiny in a small village to experiment and find his way in developing his educational ideas. He wanted to do this in a community that would be connected to the school in deep ways. A house and farm became available and this was bought with the generous funding of his brother Christoph's wife, who sold her home in Griesheim in order to make this possible.

It is difficult to know how objective the notes from pupils attending the school in 1817 might be. In other chapters of this book, consideration is given to the difficulty any institution might face in sustaining a particular approach to education in ways close to the vision of the founder. But there is some resonance between the recordings of two of the boys who boarded in Keilhau. The first was the younger brother of Heinrich Langethal, a founding teacher who helped Froebel in educating the children in the school. His younger brother, Christian Langethal clearly adored this teacher who was his older brother:

Convinced that he could educate more effectively in Keilhau, he finally decided to give up his position with the duke, disregarding the deprivation and hard work awaiting him there.(Langethal (Christian) 2016:80).

It seems that Middendorff (who became head of Keilhau after Froebel's death in 1852) introduced the boys to the ancient Greeks and Romans, and in the evenings to Schiller's ballads and poetry. Langethal took them to the middle ages and he helped them to make links with the ballads and knights of old by reading Zauberring. Significantly, Froebel agreed to order this book for them from the nearby town of Rudolstadt. Climbing the hills and in the forests surrounding Keilhau, they acted and played at being medieval knights with Langethal helping them to make helmets, breastplates, shields, learning the history as they went along. Langethal was very practical in his teaching. Middendorff required meticulous accuracy and dealt with the deep desire of the boys to be thoroughly German by requiring that they study the history of language with historic accuracy and attention to detail. Froebel, in his teaching, does not seem to have stressed the learning of facts but caused thinking in the conversations he had with the children, most of them in middle childhood. According to Christian,

> Each of our three teachers engaged us in his unique way, something we boys were encouraged to do too. They did not compete, rather they complemented one another as a team. Froebel introduced new ideas to the world, which we learned to use for our own gain. While my brother encouraged us in wild play, Middendorff created a peaceful homely atmosphere for the evenings. (Langethal, (Christian), 2016:82)

Reinhold was a boarder at a later period in the history of the school, in the period around 1910, when his father, Dr Christian Wachter, was the director. Just as Christian Langethal writes about spending time learning within the school in the mornings and then in the afternoons learning in the outdoors, making dens, or exploring the hills and forests (providing it was in hearing distance of the school bell), with the evening spent in music making, hearing the songs of Schiller, with their teachers and practical activity such as paper folding, so these traditions seem to have held across the years. Reinhold writes:

> It is strange, but school work was not important for us. At least, it was no more important than our life together, both among ourselves as pupils and with the teachers. Those were the things that mattered to us. This is part of the nature of a Froebel school. Its aim is formative and educational rather than merely academic. (Wright and Albertz, 2010:2)

Froebel's integration and interconnectivity of life and education, so that each is part of the other, beams out in this statement. Another indication that Froebel's efforts to ensure that children were 'instructed in the nature as well as the content of subjects' (Lilley, 1967:140) is shown in the fact that of two orphans who attended the schools:

> One of them became a well known and respected judge, and the other a stonemason, the creator of the monument. That children having attended the same school should become experts in such diverse fields is not surprising when one realises that Froebel believed unfailingly that every child was gifted and that each gift was of equal value. (Catalogue of the Archive Exhibition, 1982:4)

There is further evidence of the way in which the individual strengths of children were encouraged and developed in the school in that Christian Langethal became a professor of Agricultural Science at Jena University in 1872.

Communities need leaders

Sustained focus is the most important feature of a good leader. Sustained focus is something Froebel had. It brings a sense of stability and from this emerges the trust which strengthens a team and gives an understood sense of direction. It means that those joining the community realize and sign up to why and how they intend to locate themselves in their practice. Those who can see this is not their vision of life or the way to educate children and adults can leave. It releases creativity and enables free-flowing thinking. This helps to bring people into new ways of working because they are supported by feeling that they are valued in bringing about what is needed without cajolement. Froebel's way of working within the communities of practice that he established achieved this:

> Froebel surrounded himself with gifted and innovative teachers and students, leaving a group of dedicated women (and sometimes men) who identified as his disciples to more fully articulate his ideas after his death. (Prochner, 2017:2)

Robust discussions in a safe context

Being part of a close-knit community of Froebelian practice is one thing, but it certainly carries dangers of narrowness, prescription, ossification, normalization, standardization and regulation within it, as signalled by the postmodernists G. Dahlberg, P. Moss and A. Pence ([1999]2013). However, ensuring that the mature reasoning advocated by Kant is robust within the community of Froebelian practice addresses these challenges. Whether or not Froebel was aware of Kant's work, robust mature reasoning is an essential ingredient of the Froebelian communities of practice that Froebel founded in his school in Keilhau, Kindergarten in Blankenburg and other Froebelian settings thereafter. Sharing ideas with like-minded people means that arguments can become articulated with greater clarity and tried out in a supportive community without fear of being judged when they are inadequately formed. Ideas can be experimented upon, practised, and subjected to scrutiny in an atmosphere that welcomes debates and new ideas which are still emergent (Broadie, 2007). However, Froebel had seen the schisms and acrimony that developed in Pestalozzi's school in Yverdun in 1808, and was able to work in the Keilhau community such that this was avoided. Damasio's distinction between 'thoughtful feelings' and 'raw emotion' is relevant here (2004:43). Robust discussion can quickly descend into raw emotion. The mature thinking advocated by Kant chimes with the neuroscientist Damasio's concern for the necessity of 'thoughtful feelings'.

Froebel was very fortunate in building a team of people around him who helped to manage daily and difficult situations. It seems that he would leave Keilhau on their advice when relationships, funding matters and external pressures were becoming difficult, and Barop, Lanthethal and Middendorff would either accompany him or continue the work in Keilhau with unswerving devotion. This was also true of the women in the community, especially his wife Wilhelmine Henriette and his nieces. The team who were drawn to his educational approach implemented the work thoughtfully and not in prescribed forms.

Keilhau provided a relatively safe place for the Froebelian work to develop. Establishing Froebelian education beyond this location predictably proved to be hugely challenging. Foucault suggests that we need to be able to refuse the 'kind of individuality which has been imposed on us' (1980:216). The feeling that it is required and necessary to espouse the views that dominate in education was something that Froebel trained the early Kindergarten teachers not to do. This is demonstrated in the way they tirelessly continued the work after his death, as did Baroness Bertha von Marenholtz-Bulow, Bertha Ronge (who founded the first Kindergarten in Hampstead in England), her sister Margarethe Schurz (who founded the first Kindergarten in Wisconsin in the United States), Eleonore Heerwart (who was active in the Manchester Kindergarten Association and then principal of Stockwell Training College in London, also founding the British and Foreign School Society). Sustaining Froebelian practice and the thinking that supports it is something which teachers of young children find overwhelmingly difficult in English primary schools and perhaps in other countries too. They consistently report how isolated they feel, and that their educational thinking differs from that of colleagues teaching older children. Being part of a community of Froebelian practice is empowering.

Teaching children

Teaching children as individuals is not yet part of mainstream education in many places of the world. Many schools still practise instruction and schooling which is often referred to as academic studies, with breadth being provided in a limited way through expressive arts, performances from scripts, sports and gymnastics with outings to places of interest, carefully controlled through worksheets. Froebel called the rote learning, writing of texts, listening to sermons, learning hymns with moral instructions 'stone language' in a letter he wrote to the attentive and supportive Duke of Meiningen in 1827. He says in the letter that 'it takes a powerful disruptive force to break its outer covering and release the inner meaning' (Froebel in Lilley, 1967:33). Rather than giving instruction, Froebel worked with the community of teachers and the women living in the community believing that,

> True education must originate in activity and must similarly be both instructive and creative and must provide for climax and consolidation in the creative process ... There is no creative process unless one's knowledge and insight are advanced and one's life intensified; there is no move forward into knowledge unless one thinks back and preserves what is already known; there is no active life unless there is also relaxation. (Froebel in Lilley, 1967:43)

The practising of what Froebel would call 'education' (rather than 'schooling' and 'instruction') remains a huge challenge:

> I found myself at odds with all existing forms of education, and so the whole of my teaching and tutorial career was one long battle. (Froebel in Lilley, 1967:34)

Interconnected subjects

Froebel was breaking new ground, and his approach remains unusual now, in supporting children to think for themselves. An example from Stephen Moss's book (2019:35–6), *The Twelve Birds of Christmas* demonstrates the way in which education in the Froebelian sense, rather than instruction or schooling in the narrow sense, is interconnected with life. Everything links. His concept of *Unity* is always present. Turtledoves were commonly found in the UK during the late nineteenth century, as a result of new methods of arable farming which resulted in plenty of seeds for these birds to feed from during the spring and summer. By the 1980s the numbers had halved. Now they have become vulnerable and endangered.

There were droughts in the area of sub-Saharan Africa where turtle-doves spend the winter and it was argued that this caused the decline in numbers spotted in the UK during the spring and summer. But it is only when connections are made and a unified whole is pieced together that the reasons for decline emerge. Arable farming methods changed with a loss of tall, dense hedgerows for their nests, and lack of weeds with the seeds for their food. The turtledoves were unable to have two broods of chicks per year because of this. Climate change has caused the weeds and plants to bloom earlier, but the birds have not yet adapted to this so arrive back in the UK after the winter at the same time as they have done traditionally in May. They seem to be vulnerable to the parasitic disease trichomonosis. They are often shot for sport as they fly over the eastern Mediterranean, Malta, France, Spain and Italy on their return to the UK from the winter in Africa.

Froebelian education aims to cause thinking that leads to action in ways which lead to a better world. Children need to be 'instructed in the nature as well as the content of subjects' (Froebel in Lilley, 1967:140). The example of the turtledove gives insights into the nature of the subject, piecing together content so that it becomes illuminated and urgent actions are identified. Studying subjects in separated categories (environment, science, geography, and whether or not people engage respectfully with nature) lacks the sense of coordinated purpose that a good education brings. Ensuring that children and adults in the school community have a sense of *Unity* is something important to feel when visiting a school. It has been described as the 'ethos'. This cannot be measured, yet *Unity* and the ethos it promotes is a centrally important part of a school. Visitors to Keilhau, including inspectors were captivated by the atmosphere:

> It is the spirit alone which makes the school a school and the room a schoolroom, - not the ever deeper analysis of separate subjects but their coherence, as will be established if attention is directed to their inherent unity. (Froebel in Lilley, 1967:139)

The ethos of a school does not come about through the subjects that are taught. It comes about through the relationships and the atmosphere set by the leadership and the teamwork in relation to the individual, the team and the task (Adair, 2018). For Froebel the individual child (or adult) needs opportunities and support in developing their thinking and self-knowledge. This is as important as subject knowledge. The new teacher, the trainee teacher, the child or their parents,

> comes into school with the hope that here he will be taught something which he cannot learn elsewhere, that here the hunger of his mind and heart will be satisfied. (Froebel in Lilley, 1967:138)

The challenges: The Kindergarten teacher training college for women

For Froebel the important thing in training teachers was to develop practical expertise through reflective practice as a result of a high-quality training in the new training college he pioneered and, when this was thwarted, through a determined continuation of the training work in Keilhau.

One of the challenges in the early pioneering days of training Froebelian Kindergarten teachers lay in the fact that the students (mostly women but also a few men) needed to be able to see what Froebelian education looked like. As the Kindergarten movement spread, it typically became part of the practice to have a demonstration Kindergarten alongside a training college for women. The growth into this way of training Froebel teachers developed in an organic way, because lack of funding and expertise, and the demand for educational settings for children under 7 years inevitably dictated the way these provisions emerged over time.

The Froebel Educational Institute in London trained teachers emphasizing, according to Bethall (2017:54), the importance of having a philosophy of education, and the wholeness of the educational process. Observation of individual children was a key part of the training. The theories of John Dewey (1859–1952) and Sigmund Freud (1856–1939) were introduced. This was a revisionist approach, embracing Froebelian principles but not the practices which were perceived as obsolete (Bruce, 2020). L. Prochner and A. Kirova (2017:99) use the categories of Froebel training suggested by D. Snider (1900:vii–viii). A situation had developed whereby the Froebelian who founded the first, and necessarily private Kindergartens adhered closely to what had become a rigid and prescriptive use of the Froebelian materials. These Snider labels as the 'stationary' Froebelians. Froebelians pioneering the teacher training of women in the colleges were typically what Snider called 'revisionist' Froebelians. Another group continued to use the *Gifts* and *Occupations, Finger Plays and Movement Games,* but in a more flexible form, gradually adapting and changing them. These were the 'evolutionary' Froebelians.

Peter Weston suggests that,

> Essentially, the old-style Froebelians who had been running the private kindergartens were being challenged by the new educational discourse emanating from the training colleges. There would be no return to the world and authority of 'the Master' as the new century progressed. Dewey, Freud and Piaget would come irrevocably to inflect what was still known as 'Froebelianism'. (2002:31)

Y. Valkanova (2019:50) highlights the psychoanalytic Kindergartens pioneered by Vera Schmidt in Russia in post-revolutionary times. K. Bethall

(2017) describes how Maria Grey and Emily Shirriff, who founded the London-based Froebel Society, and Elizabeth Murray at Maria Grey College influenced the lectures and professional development opportunities for qualified Kindergarten teachers. Maria Findlay taught at the Froebel Educational Institute, having visited the Dewey Laboratory school in Chicago. In 1903 she wrote that

> symmetrical paper folding and symmetrical work and the gifts are a waste of time for both students and children. (Findlay, in Weston, 2002:31)

She even advised students against reading the original *Education of Man*.

The impact of this new form of Froebel training was powerful and long lasting. Interesting examples of those trained in this way are reported by Bethall (2017:52), who gathered `archival fragments' of the way in which the New Zealand context Froebelian education was transported to a colonial setting. Both Dorothy Fitch and Winifred Maitland were born and grew up in England, in middle-class homes. They both achieved the higher certificate awarded jointly from 1887 from the Froebel Educational Institute (training Kindergarten teachers from 1879) and the National Froebel Union. Typically, they then practised as teachers in Froebelian private progressive schools. Dorothy Maitland worked with Grace Owen, who also taught the Froebelian Susan Isaacs. They travelled across the world to work in New Zealand. In 1905, Dorothy Fitch became head of Kelburn Normal school which was linked to the Wellington Training College where she also taught. Winifred Maitland succeeded her in 1912. According to Bethall,

> In her ten years as Kindergarten Mistress, Maitland supported the implementation of a range of ideas drawn from the strands of developmental; psychology popular at the time. (2017:59)

Bethall admires their courage in uprooting themselves to live in a new and distant country, where they taught, not in privileged private and progressive schools but in state experimental schools. She suggests that they are also to be admired for the way in which they adapted to their new cultural context and faced the 'abundant criticism from those who did not appreciate their efforts' (Bethall, 2017:62). An example of the adjustment to the New Zealand context is in the way that,

> Maitland worked hard to gain the parents' support, encouraging their interest and involvement in school life. Whilst not willing to change her educational ideas because of criticism, she valued parental input and work in the school. In 1924 she supported plans to form a parent teacher association, one of the first in the country. (Bethall, 2017:60)

The revisionist approach to Froebel training continued becoming a 'regime of truth' (Foucault, 1980). The *Gifts* and *Occupations, Mother Songs and Movement Games* did not feature for study with a view to practical use in their original form. Nature study remained, but the original arrangement of the garden vanished. Froebelian vocabulary was dismissed as obsolete. To focus on these risked being seen as out of date, Romantic, sentimental, anti-science and anti-progress. Instead some of the materials Froebel developed as the *Occupations* (such as clay and drawing) were used in ways which linked with the 'workshop' practices together with the study of psychology, sociology and neuroscience. Topics such as 'creativity' and 'discovery' learning were introduced. Yet graduates of the Froebel Colleges continued to be proud of being Froebelians.

Still proud to be Froebelian

Ron Best writes of

the 'spirit of Froebel (at least metaphorically) being 'alive and well' and moving through the college and through our work ... So here's the puzzle: Why, in the context of a College, founded by followers of Froebel and still bearing his name, with many presenters from the College itself, was there, over ten years of conferences, so little reference to the man himself? Why was he not central to the discussion?(Best, 2016:2)

The revisionist trained Froebelians dominated the field from the turn of the nineteenth century until recently. Dissemination through teacher training in colleges in the UK through those settling in colonially linked countries such as New Zealand (May 2017) and India (Read, 2018)) is one feature. The revisionist work in the United States is another strand. Prochner and Kirova (2017:99) examine the work of Anna Bryan and Elizabeth Harrison. The way in which these two Froebelians worked demonstrates the importance of who trains who in the Froebelian canon of practice. Bryan led the Chicago Free Kindergarten Association (CFKA) and was a revisionist. Harrison led the Chicago Kindergarten College and was more evolutionary. Susan Blow, working in the St Louis Kindergartens she founded, was stationary. As Prochner and Kirova put it:

Thus those who resisted the introduction of new materials, or reinterpretation of old materials, along with changes to philosophy and teacher preparation, were criticised for delaying the revolution – that is educational change. (2017:100)

Practitioner networks: Then

Earlier in the chapter the importance of Kindergartens offering train-ing for Froebelians in the context of Kindergarten training colleges was introduced. In this way, practice was not separated from the training. Kristen Nawrotzki (2017:91) argues that the closure of the Grand Rapids Kindergarten Training School (GRKS), Michigan, in 1919 came at a point when there was a need for more locally accessible support and training. This Kindergarten had served an important role in supporting Froebelian prac-tice but could no longer achieve this as Kindergarten teachers were increas-ingly too distant geographically with the expanding numbers. The existence of private and free Kindergartens depends on donors, or parents being able to pay fees. Funding issues bring vulnerability. But they can forge a trail for public funded Kindergartens. This was the case with the Grand Rapids Kindergarten:

> Widespread adoption of public school kindergartening was the result of the kindergarten movement's success. (Nawrotzki, 2017:91)

Froebel networks formed for several reasons. These include the devel-opment of public funding for Kindergartens in different countries during the 1920s; the presence of recently trained Kindergarten teachers; evidence emerging from the new discipline of psychology; health services developing; the child study movement. Kristen Nawrotzki writes of the early Froebel networks:

> These networks were based on extensive and intensive communica-tion between individuals, groups and – increasingly – institutions, whether by individual correspondence, periodical publication or travel. (2017:93)

Powerful Froebelian networks still form now (Bruce, 2020; Bruce, Elfer and Powell, 2019:202; Bruce, Hakkarainen and Bredikyte, 2017:9–22). Nawrotzki argues that this enabled Kindergartens to find teachers who were trained in Froebelian ideals. It gave opportunities to broadcast the excellent work they were doing. This continues today. Froebelians learn from each other's examples and arrange to visit schools and settings. There is now the added advantage of technology which allows meetings by digital means, and rapid interchange of thoughts, challenges, discussion and collaborative efforts in finding ways forward. Nawrotzki calls this the culture of travel and exchange which has taken on new forms and possibilities in today's world. Bethall also sees Froebelian networks as important in the sustaining and developing of early childhood education. Networks and relationships established modern professional identities within a gendered world that offered women new opportunities but left them still bound by traditional ideas. (Bethall, 2017:52)

In this sense, Froebel's active work to bring about the possibility for women to have intellectual lives and to become qualified professional teachers succeeded, but attitudes to the role of women on a larger scale were still a long way from being established (Steedman, 1985). Nawrotzki argues that there is both 'the importance of individual and the power of networks in effecting change at a local level'(2017:92). She gives a central place to 'local heroes', as she describes them, and she names Lucretia Willard Treat, Clara Wheeler, Emma Field and Constance Rourke, all active in the Grand Rapids Kindergarten Association.

Froebelian Networks: Now

A detailed description of the emergence of the Edinburgh Froebel Network forms a chapter in the *Routledge International Handbook of Froebel and Early Childhood Practice: Re-articulating Research and Policy* (Bruce, Elfer and Powell, 2019:231–44). In Edinburgh, the head teacher of five maintained nursery schools in Edinburgh – Maureen Baker, Stella Brown, Catriona Gill, Chris McCormick, and Jane Whinnett – and the head of the Centre for Children Under Fives and their families, Lynn McNair, came together through the powerful process of happenstance. Jane Whinnett likens this to the strawberry plant and its runners. It is a question of one thing leading to another and a case of things happening in the right place, at the right time in the right way. This has resulted in the development of a certificate course in Froebelian practice at the University of Edinburgh together with a BA in Early Childhood Studies and MSc with Froebel pathways taught by this team. There are annual conferences attended by about two hundred and fifty delegates, some practitioners and some academics and policy makers. The eleventh conference (for three days) hosts the International Froebel Society in Edinburgh.

There have been two books, one prize winning, *Early Childhood Practice: Froebel Today* (Bruce, 2012) and *Putting Storytelling at the Heart of Early Childhood Practice: a reflective guide for early years practitioners* (Bruce, McNair and Whinnett, 2020). A number of articles have been published at regular intervals. The network leaders have given seminars, keynote lectures at international and national conferences, and organized master classes for alumni of the Edinburgh University Froebel courses. There are cultural exchange visits with other Froebelians. None of this would have developed without these 'local heroes'. The strawberry runners have linked with another powerful Froebelian network led by Mark and Debby Hunter who are head teachers of the Annan school in East Sussex, which follows a Froebelian approach. This, the Froebel Network, encourages digital discussion between Froebelians. There is an annual Froebel gathering in for those who have studied on Froebel courses. This is closely linked to the Froebel Trust who give generous support and encouragement.

These recent examples chime with the picture Nawrotzki drew of the early Froebel Network at the Grand Rapids Kindergarten Association in Michigan. The same themes of action are there. The Froebelian Networks continue, arising as happenstance dictates and with strawberry runners in different parts of the world but in a modern form. However, there is one development which is an important part of the Froebelian Networks which needs to be highlighted. This is the importance of practical Froebelian training. Previously, it was possible for teachers to take the National Froebel Union Certificate locally with the award centrally administered in Manchester Square in London until 1964 (Scacchi, 2019b:40).

Reconnectionist Froebel training courses today

In 2010, members of the Froebel Trust Education Committee reported that although practitioners deeply value opportunities to study on accredited Froebel courses, they would also welcome short, highly practical short courses taught to the whole staff in their setting so that this could become a community of Froebelian practice. A pilot, led by the author who gathered a development team, was undertaken with the thirteen Yellow Dot day nurseries in Hampshire, led by Jane Dyke and her deputy Paula Phillips. Feedback from Yellow Dot gave invaluable guidance on how to offer the courses. Dr Stella Louis leads a group of apprentice Travelling Tutors. Guildford Maintained Nursery school and Children's Centre were the first to complete all five Elements and are now disseminating reconnected Froebelian practices and principles.

These courses, and the accredited Froebel courses at the universities of Edinburgh and Roehampton, are helping Froebelians working in the UK and beyond to unearth buried treasure and to think their way into how they wish to work with children in the culture and contexts in which they operate. The interconnectivity internationally is also proving important, just as it has always done for the Froebelian transglobal arena. Dissemination of Froebelian practice in reconnected forms in different parts of the world through publications, supporting conferences, Froebel Trust endorsed courses is moving to Froebelians inviting researchers to work with them. An important aspect of these developments is the grassroot communities of practice which are forming as the Froebel Practitioner Networks of the future in the UK, South Africa (Cape Town and Johannesburg) Kolkata and Western Australia.

The first Froebelian community of practice

Froebel's approach held in great respect the views of his team leaders, including his wife Wilhelmine Henriette Hoffmeister – to whom he was married in 1818 and who supported his work until her death in 1839 – and the teachers Wilhelm Middendorf and Heinrich Langethal who joined the school in Keilhau in 1817, followed by Johannes Barop in 1826. His second wife Luise Levin, whom he married in 1851, the year before his death, was important in supporting his work as a staff member in the community and after his death in taking forward his legacy (including his desk, which is now in the museum in Blankenburg with a book by Goethe on the shelf above it). Reflective practice was the key to this community working together around shared values. In this sense his work was more in tune with the reasoning and rationalism of the Enlightenment approach than the emotional, solitary and individualist approach of a Romantic. He was also typical of Enlightenment thinkers in that he did not hide in the safe haven of Keilhau:

> Froebel worked tirelessly in promoting the kindergarten system. He lobbied local official and parents all over the German states, and by 1850 sixteen had been established, together with a number of training centres for young women as 'kindergartners'. (Weston, 2002:2)

Robust discussions and promotion of Froebelian education

Once the arguments for a point of view and approach to work became sufficiently developed, he and his community of trained Froebelians

> committed their writings to the public domain, discussed and disputed with each other in public, and did so in freedom: in the sense that they were not constrained by fear of what might become of them if their ideas met with the disapproval of the political, religious, or other authorities. (Broadie 2007:20).

This allows educational ideas and their practical implementation to be debated and argued with those less like-minded who will take a great deal of convincing. By 1850, when the Duke of Meiningen donated a building for the training of Kindergartners, Froebel had developed a whole vocabulary of educational terms, together with practical materials and the principles which supported this. The devastating blow when the Prussian government issued the Verbot (1851), closing the Kindergartens had an extraordinary impact:

Repressive and totalitarian measures, however, often have unexpected results. Many German kindergartners who were committed to Froebel's ideals moved abroad to England, Ireland and many other countries of Europe, as well as the USA.(Weston, 2002:2).

By the time Froebel died in 1852, the groundwork was sufficiently strong for Froebelian education to be sustained in different parts of the world. How stationary, evolutionary or revolutionary (revisionist) Froebelian practices became, what remains and what is beginning to burgeon has been a focus of this chapter. What is clear in every chapter of this book is that the time is ripe for the new assemblage of reconnected Froebelian thinking. The principles with the practices of Froebelian education have been separated for too long in the revisionist tradition (Bruce, Hakkarainen and Bredikyte, 2017; Bruce, Elfer and Powell, 2019; Bruce, 2020).

The Froebelian principles and practices reconnected

The revisionist Froebelians emphasized the Froebelian principles. For those trained in this spirit there was nevertheless an intuition that these needed to be overtly stated, albeit in modern-day language:

1. Childhood is seen as valid in itself, as part of life and not simply as preparation for adulthood. Thus, education is seen similarly as something of the present and not just preparation and training for later.

2. The whole child is considered to be important. Health, physical and mental, is emphasized, as well as the importance of feelings, thinking and spiritual aspects.

3. Learning is not compartmentalized, for everything links.

4. Intrinsic motivation, resulting in child-initiated, self -directed activity, is valued.

5. Self-discipline is valued.

6. There are specially receptive periods of learning at different stages of development.

7. What children can do (rather than what they cannot do) is the starting point in the child's education.

8. There is an inner symbolic life in the child that emerges especially under favourable conditions.

9. The people (both adults and children) with whom the child interacts are of central importance.

10. The child's education is seen as an interaction between the child and the environment in which the child finds her/himself – including, in particular, other people and knowledge itself.

(Bruce, 1987; Bruce, 2020)

Principle 1 links with Froebel's concept of *becoming* and the contribution of education from birth throughout life. At every stage, be that stage without hurrying children into adulthood.

Principle 2 sees the whole child as part of the concept of *Unity* and the interconnectivity of whole body, health, feelings, ideas, thoughts as well as relationships and spirituality.

Principle 3 emphasizes the need to link, always linking subject knowledge through the *Forms* of *Everyday life, Beauty* and *Knowledge.*

Principle 4 focuses on the *self-activity* of the child. *Freedom with guidance* is of central importance in supporting children. Children's natural disposition is that they want to learn about the world they inhabit, with the people they meet and those beyond.

Principle 5 shows how children are fundamentally good and want to contribute to a better world. They appreciate *freedom with guidance.* They explore the *law of opposites.* Given opportunities they will joyously and seriously engage with nature.

Principle 6 links to the way Froebel believed that *at every stage they should be that stage* and that good teaching matches where the child is in their learning and builds on this. *Observation* therefore matters, so that teaching does not use stone language with little meaning or joy for the child.

Principle 7 says to begin where the learner is, not where you want them to be, or they ought to be.

Principle 8 deals with the *symbolic life* of the child and the *inner* becoming *outer* and the *outer* becoming *inner.* The *law of opposites* is important in this.

Principle 9 Froebel placed great emphasis on the nurture of children and empowerment of the intellectual life through relationships. Family and nurturing school environments are basic to children wanting to learn.

Principle 10 connects the self-awareness of the child with participation and contribution to the community and the world of nature and universe, as the child's knowledge develops. Everything is linked. *Unity* is at the heart of Froebelian education. Each of these principles provide the means to link with different aspects of his thinking.

But without the practice they are general and beg the question, what does Froebelian education look like and feel like in practice?

As this book is going to the press a reconnected pamphlet 'Froebel's Principles and Practices' is being written by Helen Tovey (to be published by the Froebel Trust, 2020)

The children

In a mixed nursery/reception class of a primary school in England, clay, a Froebelian *Occupation,* was introduced to a group of 3 and 4-year-olds. The children were invited to put on pinafores, and to roll up their sleeves. Here was *freedom with guidance.* Some children did this independently. Others did not or could not. The adults did not require independence and willingly helped children who asked. One child had used clay before, at home. For the others it was a new experience. Two adults sat with the children, who could come and go as they wished. Three or four stayed for an hour. Adults began pinching clay, pushing thumbs into it, rolling it, bashing it to flatten it. The little girl who had used clay before made a thumb pot, and a coil pot and offered children pretend drinks. Here was *self-activity,* using one of the *Occupations.* Several children began rolling or bashing the clay, simply enjoying the experience, Others made insects, birds, nests, plates, and interacted with the adults, who pinched legs out of lumps. Animals began to live in the caves they made, or the fields they bashed and flattened, or were fenced in with lumps of clay. One little boy looked in amazement when the adult showed him the pot the little girl had made and suggested the tortoise she had made might like a drink. He roared with laughter and was clearly shocked and delighted. Not all the children used English as their first language, but they helped each other to express themselves, enjoy, struggle and share with the English-speaking adults.

Froebel's advice, *at every stage be that stage,* is echoed. Children at this time of childhood are becoming *symbol users* and *symbol makers.* The focus is on what children can do, and is not about deficit. This was a whole experience, with the *Forms* as a central part. Children connected to *everyday* experiences of animals and crockery, visiting parks and the city farm they visit with school. They were struck with what they could make with the clay. There is *Beauty* in the objects and animals that children see they have brought into a tangible form. Seeing an idea take shape has *Beauty.* They acquired *scientific knowledge* of the properties of clay, and vocabulary. They acquired *social knowledge* learning with and through other children and adults. The little boy learnt that you can represent things in clay. The *symbolic life* emerged. The conditions were favourable. This is a learning *community* in which the way people interact with each other matters. Adults are *observing* and learning what children can do and thinking how to help them appropriately in educationally worthwhile ways.

Reconnection

This book advocates that the revisionist stage in the Froebelian journey is replaced with a period of reconnection. There is interconnectivity at the core of his concept of *Unity* through the *reconnection* of Froebel's principles and practices. There is a burgeoning future for *reconnecting Froebelians* and important work to do with children and their families.

REFLECTIONS

This is a book about reconnection between the principles and practices of Froebel's vision of education. The revisionist approach, emphasizing Froebelian principles rather than the practices, which has come to dominate the last two centuries has been a very valuable part of the Froebelian journey, since Froebel's death in 1852. It has caused a great deal of useful and worthwhile thinking for practitioners. It has meant the shedding of ossified and by-the-book ways of using his educational framework. It has challenged to a degree the natural inclination to cherry-pick and take what is attractive, letting other elements wither and fade away. While it has not been a waste of time, a great deal has been lost. Or perhaps, it is best to describe this as much has been buried. Thanks to the stalwart work of Froebelian scholars beavering away to find archival remnants, it is becoming increasingly possible to see through a lens of historic exploration more than was possible before. What emerges is the necessity of using Froebel's whole framework, the thought-provoking principles and the way the thoughts connect to the practice.

Threaded through the book are important phrases of Froebelian vocabulary which, when used in today's context, bring alive his practices. The way the experiences of his childhood led him to emphasize the importance of nurture, and how this influenced his focus on the relationship between nature and children is of central importance. The growth and development of the child are fundamental to both. Creating contexts and conditions for both to flourish are key to whether or not gardens or children flourish. Family life is part of this, and he concentrates on how to be idealistic in this, rather than taking a deficit approach and dwelling on what might go wrong. He can be challenged for using sentimental metaphors, or for being unrealistic in his vision.

He is not someone who tries to make everyone he works with or the children he teaches or his friends, think in the same way as he does. *Unity* is about self-awareness, and being part of and contributing to the immediate community and to what lies beyond in nature, the world of people, the universe. He is inclusive, conventional and yet, very individual in his thinking. He can be accused of being muddled, or, as the end of the first chapter suggests, he manages to bring disparate things together into an interconnected whole against what logic might predict. But he is not all things to all people.

Some people are drawn to being Froebelians. Others are not. The fact that his work is still being used and explored in the transglobal arena suggests that there is more to this than is simple.

Leadership is about sustaining a vision and sticking to bringing the idea to fruition through adversity and challenge. It means bringing people with you, and his community at Keilhau was hugely important in this. The men's names are better known, but a bit of delving reveals the important contribution of the women. He believed that education is about causing thought and making a better world. His colleagues in the community of Froebelian practice embraced this. So do Froebelians today. It is no easier to take forward his practice now than it was then. There is no Verbot, but school and other settings have structures and systems in different parts of the world that still make it very difficult to be a fully functioning Froebelian in everyday practice. There is determination to support children to feel good about their learning and recognize their efforts in sensitive, long-lasting ways, to encourage their thinking, imagination and creativity and to make connections working from whole to parts (rather than gather fragmented parts to try and make a whole).

The value of the garden and landscapes can be dismissed as a sentimental metaphor, or seen as being of central importance in tackling the enormous challenges of climate change. Issues of urban and rural life are part of this debate. The *freedom and guidance* that is part of using the tangibles of Froebel's curriculum framework are important, with an interactionist approach at the heart. The *Gifts* and *Occupations* are tangible, but there is a problem with tangibility when people try to pin children down to a specific use which constrains their thinking. Alternatively, they might simply present children with the tangible materials, leaving them without the adult's interest in how they use them which also constrains the thinking of the children. There are problems with both the transmission and laissez-faire approaches when tangible materials are offered to children. Relationships matter to Froebel, whether while walking in the countryside or in streets with a group of children, or singing songs together. Cultivating the *inner* thoughts and the *outer* expression as different aspects of the *symbolic life* of the child is an important part of teaching.

Froebel was a cutting-edge scientist studying crystallography, and added what he learnt about observation in that role to what he gained from the time he spent with Pestalozzi. He observed and built his curriculum around what he realized was important to children, their interests, their play, their need for nurture and the encouraging of physical learning, and the *Forms* of their *Everyday lives, Beauty and Knowledge*. I still want to be a Froebelian, while recognizing that there are many aspects of his way of working and thinking which are open to challenge. His principles matter, but they need to connect to the practice. In putting together in 1987 the Froebelian principles expressed in modern language (Chapter Eight), it was clear to me that those working in Montessori or Steinerian frameworks would agree with these. But when it comes to practice, there would be differences in the way of practical working with children.

Whom have you learned to know on your journey?

Froebel, 1897:246

I have learned, through my Froebelian journey, to value *Unity*, the interconnected core of Froebel's thinking. Reconnection matters.

REFERENCES

Adair, J. (2018), *Lessons in Leadership*. London: Bloomsbury.

Allport, G. W. (1967), *The Individual and His Religion: A Psychological Interpretation*. London: Constable.

Aspin, D. (1983), 'Friedrich Froebel: Visionary, Prophet and Healer?' *Early Childhood Education and Care*, 12 (3 and 4): 247–77.

Athey, C. (1990), *Extending Thought in Young Children: A Parent Teacher Partnership*. London: Paul Chapman.

Bakker, N. (2017), 'Happiness, Play and Bourgeois Morality: The Early Years of Froebel Schooling in the Netherlands, 1858–1904', in P. May, K. Nawrotzki and L. Prochner (eds), *Kindergarten Narratives on Froebelian Education: Transnational Investigations,* 35–51. London: Bloomsbury.

Bartholomew, L. and T. Bruce (1994), *Getting to Know You: A Guide to Record-keeping in Early Childhood Education and Care*. London: Hodder and Stoughton.

Best, R. (2016), 'Exploring the Spiritual in the Pedagogy of Friedrich Froebel', 15th International Conference on Children's Spirituality, Spirituality and the Whole Child: Interdisciplinary Approaches, 1–22, Lincoln: Bishop Grosseteste University, 26–27 July.

Bethall, K. (2017), 'Froebelian Teachers Abroad: Implementing a Modern Infant Education System in Colonial Wellington, New Zealand, 1906–25', in P. May, K.Nawrotzki and L. Prochner (eds), *Kindergarten Narratives on Froebelian Education: Transnational Investigations,* 51–66. London: Bloomsbury.

Bethall, K. (2019), 'Transnational Froebelian Travelling Teachers', in T. Bruce, P. Elfer and S. Powell with L. Werth (eds), *The Routledge International Handbook of Froebel and Early Childhood Practice: Re-articulating Research and Policy,* 179–82. London: Routledge.

Bloomfield, A. (2000), '"Mrs Roadknight Reports …": Jane Roadknight's Visionary Role in Transforming Elementary Education', in M. Hilton and P. Hirsch (eds), *Practical Visionaries: Women, Education and Social Progress 1790–1930,* 167–82. Harlow: Pearson Education.

Bradburn, E. (1989), *Portrait of a Pioneer*. London: Routledge.

Bredikyte, M. (2017), 'Introduction', in T. Bruce, M. Bredikyte and P. Hakkarinen (eds), *The Routledge International Handbook of Early Childhood Play.* 3–5, London: Routledge.

Brehony, K. (2000), 'English Revisionist Froebelians and the Schooling of the Urban Poor', in M. Hilton and P. Hirsch (eds), *Practical Visionaries: Women, Education and Social Progress 1790–1930,* 183–201. Harlow: Pearson Education.

Brehony, K. (2017), 'Working at Play or Playing at Work? A Froebelian Paradox Re-examined', in P. May, K. Nawrotzki and L. Prochner with L. Werth (eds),

The Routledge International Handbook of Froebel and Early Childhood Practice: Re-articulating Research and Policy, 15–14. London: Routledge.

Broadie, A. (2007), *The Scottish Enlightenment.* Edinburgh: Birlinn.

Brosterman, N. (1997), *Inventing Kindergarten.* New York: Harry N. Abrams.

Brown, S. (2012), 'The Changing of the Seasons in the Child Garden', in T. Bruce (ed.), *Early Childhood Practice: Froebel Today,* 29–43. London: Sage.

Bruce, I. (2013), *Charity Marketing: Delivering Income, Services and Campaigns,* 3rd edn. London: nstitute of Chartered Secretaries and Administrators.

Bruce, T. (1987), *Early Childhood Education* (5th edn. 2015). London: Hodder and Stoughton.

Bruce, T. (1991), *Time to Play in Early Childhood Education.* London: Hodder and Stoughton.

Bruce, T. (1992), [Film] *Building the Future.* Roehampton: TVR.

Bruce, T. (1996), *Helping Young Children to Play.* London: Hodder Education.

Bruce, T. (2004), *Developing Learning in Early Childhood.* London: Sage.

Bruce, T. (2011), *Cultivating Creativity: For Babies, Toddlers and Young Children,* 2nd edn. London: Hodder Education.

Bruce, T. (ed.) (2012), *Early Childhood Practice: Froebel Today.* London: Sage.

Bruce, T. (2015), *Early Childhood Education,* 5th edn. London: Hodder Education.

Bruce, T. (2017), 'Ponderings on Play: Froebelian Assemblages', in T. Bruce, M. Bredikyte and P. Hakkarainen (eds), *The Routledge International Handbook of Early Childhood Play,* 9–22, London: Routledge.

Bruce, T. (2020), *Educating Young Children: A Lifetime Journey into a Froebelian Approach: The Selected Works of Tina Bruce.* London: Routledge.

Bruce, T. and J. Dyke (2017a), 'Learning from Froebel: The Gifts', *Nursery World,* 23 January–5 February: 27–30.

Bruce, T. and J. Dyke (2017b), 'Learning from Froebel: Occupations', *Nursery World,* 20 February–5 March: 27–30.

Bruce, T. and J. Dyke (2017c), 'The Symbolic Life of the Child', *Nursery World,* 17–30 April: 25–9.

Bruce, T. and J. Dyke (2017d), 'Learning from Froebel: The Place of Nature in Learning', *Nursery World,* 20 March–2 April: 23–5.

Bruce, T. and J. Dyke (2017e), 'The Importance of Nurture', *Nursery World,* 18May–2 June: 24–7.

Bruce, T. and J. Dyke (2017f), 'Intrinsic Motivation', *Nursery World,* 26 June–9 July: 25–8.

Bruce, T. and S. Louis (2019), 'Froebelian Work in South Africa', in T. Bruce, P. Elfer and S. Powell (eds), *The Routledge International Handbook of Froebel and Early Childhood Practice: Re-articulating Research and Policy,* 245–51. London: Routledge.

Bruce, T. and J. Spratt (2011), *The Essentials of Literacy: A Whole-child Approach to Communication, Language and Literacy.* 2nd edn. London: Sage.

Bruce, T., P. Elfer and S. Powell (eds) (2019), *The Routledge International Handbook of Froebel and Early Childhood Practice: Re-articulating Research and Policy.* London: Routledge.

Bruce, T., P. Hakkarainen and M. Bredikyte (eds) (2017), *The Routledge International Handbook of Early Childhood Play.* London: Routledge.

Bruce, T., S. Louis and G. McCall (2014), *Observing Young Children.* London: Sage.

Bruce, T., L. McNair and J. Whinnett (eds) (2020), *Putting Storytelling at the Heart of Early Chioldhood Practice: A Reflective Guide for Early Years Practitioners.* London: Routledge.

Bruner, J. (1977), *The Process of Education,* 3rd edn. Cambridge, MA: Harvard University Press.

Catalogue of the Archive Exhibition (1982), *The Bicentenary of the Birth of Friedrich Froebel 1782–1982.* London: Froebel Institute College.

Community Playthings (2016), *Keilhau: Froebel's Valley of Education,* trans. Verlag Friedrick Frommann, from Keilhau in seinen Anfangen. Erinnerungen des altesten Zoglings der Anstalt, Jena 1867, Archives of the Frie Frobelschule: Community Playthings.

Dahlberg, G., P. Moss and A. Pence ([1999]2013), *Beyond Quality in Early Childhood Education and Care: Post-modern Perspectives.* Oxford: Routledge.

Damasio, A. (2004), *Looking for Spinoza.* London: Vintage.

Davies, M. (2003), *Movement and Dance in Early Childhood Education,* 2nd edn, London: Paul Chapman.

Dearden, R. (1968), *The Philosophy of Primary Education.* London: Routledge and Kegan Paul.

Denton, A. and L. Parker (n.d.), *Cooking with Young Children.* London: Froebel Trust.

Dewey, J. (1990), *The School and Society and the Child and the Curriculum.* Chicago: University of Chicago Press (Copyright at the University of Chicago, 1900 and 1902 respectively).

Department for Education and Skills/QCA (2000), *Curriculum Guidance for the Foundation Stage.* London: Department for Education and Skills.

Department for Education and Skills/QCA (2002), *Birth to Three Matters: A Framework to Support Children in Their Earliest Years* London: Department for Education and Skills: Sure Start Unit.

Dommel, C. (2004), 'Froebel's Potential for Religious Pluralism – Religion in Germany in Early Childhood Pedagogy', *Early Childhood Practice: The Journal for Multi Professional Partnerships,* 6 (2): 35–47.

Dyke, J. (2017), 'Learning from Froebel: Nature', *Nursery World* (20 March–2 April): 23–5.

Dyke, J. (n.d.), *Songs, Rhymes and Finger Plays: Exploring Froebel's Mother-Play and Nursery Songs.* London: Froebel Trust.

El Gemayel, S. (2020), 'Childhood and Play "In-between": Young Irqui and Syrian Child Refugees' Play in Lebanon', PhD diss., UCL, Institute of Education.

Flewitt, R. and K. Cowan (2020), *Valuing Young Children's Signs of Learning: Observation and Digital Documentation of Play in Early Years Classrooms.* London: Froebel Trust.

Foucault, M. (1980), *Power/Knowledge: Selected Interviews and Other Writings, 1972–1977.* Brighton: Harvester Press.

Froebel, F. (1826), *The Education of Man,* trans. W. N. Hailman. New York: Appleton.

Froebel. F. (1844), *Mutter und Koselieder* [Mother Play and Nursery Songs]. Boston: Lee Shepherd.

Froebel, F. (1891), *Letters on the Kindergarten,* trans. and annotated by E. Michaelis and H. Keatley Moore. London: Swann Sonnenschein.

Froebel, F. (1895a), *Mottoes and Commentaries of Friedrich Froebel's Mother Play,* trans. H. R. Eliot and S. E. Blow. New York: Appleton.

Froebel, F. (1895b), *Mother Songs, Games and Stories* [the Mother Song Book] trans. F. and E. Lord. London: William Rice.

Froebel, F. ([1861])1897), *Pedagogics of the Kindergarten,* trans. J. Jarvis, London: Edward Arnold.

Froebel, F. (1899), *Education by Development: The Second Part of the Pedagogics of the Kindergarten,* trans. J. Jarvis, reprint (1905). New York: D. Appleton.

Froebel. F. (1912), *Chief Educational Writings,* trans. S. Fletcher and J. Welton. London: Edward Arnold.

Froebel, F. ([1886] 1915), *Autobiography of Friedrich Froebel,* trans. E. Michaelis and H. Moore. London: Swan Sonnenschein.

Froebel, F. (1929), *Extracts from Letters Written by Friedrich Froebel,* E. Murray (ed.), trans. E. Michaelis and H. Keatley Moore in 1891 (original ed. H. Poesche). London: Froebel Society.

Goddard-Blythe, S. (2004), *The Well Balanced Child: Movement and Early Learning* Stroud: Hawthorne Press.

Guanella, F. (1934), 'Blockbuilding Activities of Young Children', *Archives of Psychology,* 174: 48–58.

Gura, P. (ed.) (1992), *Exploring Learning: Young Children and Blockplay,* London: Paul Chapman.

Harding, S. (2001), 'What's Happening with the Bikes?' *Early Childhood Practice: The Journal for Multi Professional Partnerships,* 3 (2): 24–41.

Harding, S. and F. Thomas (2020), *Growing a Nursery School from Seed.* London: Froebel Trust.

Herrington, S. (1998), 'The Garden in Froebel's Kindergarten: Beyond the Metaphor', *Studies in the History of Gardens and Designed Landscapes,* 18 (4): 326–38.

Herrington, S. (2001), 'Kindergarten: Garden Pedagogy from Romanticism to Reform', *Landscape Journal: Design, Planning and Management of Land,* 20 (1): 30–47.

Hirsch, S. (ed.) (1984), *The Block Book.* Washington, DC: National Association of Education for Young Children.

Hilton, M. and Hirsch, P. (eds) (2000), *Practical Visionaries: Women, Education and Social Progress 1790–1930.* Harlow: Pearson Education.

Holroyd, S. (2014), 'Froebel's Gifts and Blockplay in the Development of Free Play in a Nabadisha School in Kolkata', *Early Education Journal,* 72 (Spring): 8–9.

Holroyd, S., T. Miller, F. Thomas, J. Leyburg, K. Razzall and A. Dutta (2019), 'The Froebel Trust Kolkata Project', in T. Bruce, P. Elfer and S. Powell with L. Werth (eds), *The Routledge International Handbook of Froebel and Early Childhood Practice: Re-articulating Research and Policy,* 105–13. London: Routledge.

Hoskins, L. and S. Smedley (2020), 'Tina Bruce (b.1947): Advocating and Practising Froebelian Principles', in A. Palmer and J. Read, British Froebelian Women from the Mid-nineteenth to the Twentiy-first Century: A Community of Progressive Educators. 165-180, London: Routledge.

Hughes, A. and J. Cousins (2017), 'Play Birth to Three: Treasure Baskets and Heuristic Play, the Legacy of Elinor Goldschmied (1910–2009)', in T. Bruce, P. Hakkarainen and M. Bredikyte (eds), *The Routledge International Handbook of Early Childhood Play,* 33–45. London: Routledge.

Isaacs, S. (1930), *Intellectual Growth in Young Children*. London: Routledge and Kegan Paul.

Isaacs, S. (1933), *Social Development in Young Children*. London: Routledge and Kegan Paul.

Jebb, E. Mary (1953), *The Significance of Froebel's Ethical Teaching for Today, (The Claude Montefiore Lecture), np*. London: Liberal Jewish Synagogue.

Johnson, H. (1933), 'The Art of Blockbuilding', rep. E. Provenzo (Jnr) and A. Brett (1983), *The Complete Block Book*. Syracuse: Syracuse University Press.

Kalliala, M. (2006), *Play Culture in a Changing World*. Maidenhead: Open University Press.

Kant, I. ([1781] 1999), *A Critique of Pure Reason*, trans. A. Wood. Cambridge: Cambridge University Press.

Konrad, C. (2010), 'Notes from a Workshop on the Mother Songs', 1–17, Jena: International Froebel Society Conference.

Khulman, K. and L. Schweinhart (1999), *Music, Movement and Timing*. Ypsilanti MI: High Scope Educational Research Foundation.

Kretzman, J. and J. McKnight (1993), *Building Communities from the Inside Out: A Path towards Finding and Mobilising a Community's Assets*. Chicago: ACTA.

Langethal, C. (2016), 'Early Keilhau: Memories of Froebel's First Boarding Student Dr. C. Langethal', in Community Playthings, *Keilhau – Froebel's Valley of Education*, trans. from Keilhau in seinen Anfangen. Erinnerungen des altesten Zoglings der Anstalt. Jena 1867. Verlag Friedr. Frommann. With kind permission of the Archives of the Freie Frobelschule, Keilhau. Part II, 67–105.

Law, S. (2007), *Philosophy*. London: Dorling Kindersley.

Lawrence, E. (1952), *Froebel and English Education*. London: National Froebel Foundation.

Liebschner, J. (1985), 'Children Learning Through Each Other', *Early Child Development and Care*, 21: 121–34.

Liebschner, J. ([1992] 2001), *A Child's Work: Freedom and Guidance in Froebel's Educational Theory and Practice*. Cambridge: Lutterworth.

Lilley, Irene M. (1967), *Friedrich Froebel: A Selection from His Writings*. Cambridge: Cambridge University Press.

Malloch, S. and C. Trevarthen (2009), 'Musicality: Communicating the Vitality and Interests of Life', in S. Malloch and C. Trevarthen (eds), *Communicative Musicality: Exploring the Basis of Human Companionship*, 1–16. Oxford: Oxford University Press.

Matthews, J. (2003), *Drawing and Painting: Children's Visual Representation*, 2nd edn. London: Sage.

May, H. (2017), 'Relocation, Continuity and Change: Dunedin Kindergartens, Aotearoa New Zealand', in H. May, K. Nawrotzki and L. Prochner (eds), *Kindergarten Narratives on Froebelian Education: Transnational Investigations*, 167–80. London: Bloomsbury.

May, H., K. Nawrotzki and L. Prochner (eds) (2017), *Kindergarten Narratives on Froebelian Education: Transnational Investigation*. London: Bloomsbury.

McCormick, C. (2012), 'Froebelian Methods in the Modern World: A Case of Cooking', in T. Bruce (ed.), *Early Childhood Practice: Froebel Today*, 137–54. London: Sage.

McMillan, M. (1930), *The Nursery School*. London: Dent.

McNair, L. (2007), 'A Developmental Project in the Garden', *Early Childhood Practice: The Journal for Multi Professional Partnerships*, 9 (1): 31–41.

McNair, L. (2012), 'Offering Children First-hand Experiences through Forest School', in T. Bruce (ed.), *Early Childhood Practice: Froebel Today*, 57–68, London: Sage.

Mollenhauer, K. (1991), 'Finger Plays: A Pedagogical Reflection', *Phenomenology and Pedagogy*, 9: 286–300.

Moore, T. W. (1974), *Educational Theory: An Introduction*. London: Routledge and Kegan Paul.

Moorhouse, P. (2018), *Learning through Woodwork: Introducing Woodwork in the Early Years*. London: Routledge.

Moss, S. (2019), *The Twelve Birds of Christmas*. London: Penguin.

Murray, E. (ed.) (1929), *Extracts from Letters Written by Friedrich Froebel*, trans. E. Michaelis and H. Keatley Moore in 1891 (original editor H. Poesche). London: Froebel Society.

Nawrotzki, K. (2017), '"Such Marvellous Training": Grand Rapids, Michigan as a Kindergartening Centre, 1870–1905', in H. May, K. Nawrotzki and L. Prochner (eds), *Kindergarten Narratives on Froebelian Education: Transnational Investigations*, 81–98. London: Bloomsbury.

Nawrotzki, K. (2019), 'Froebel Is Dead: Long Live Froebel! The National Froebel Foundation and English Education', in T. Bruce, P. Elfer and S. Powell (eds), *The Routledge International Handbook of Froebel and Early Childhood Practice: Re-articulating Research and Policy*, 57–67. London: Routledge.

Niemela, R., A. Reichstein and T. Sillanpaa (2019), *The Miraculous Ball: Cube, Cylinder and the Other Fun Shapes in the World*. Helsinki: Ebeneser Foundation, Kindergarten Museum.

Nishida, Y. (2014), '"Come, Let Us Live with Our Children!" The Kindergarten's Arrival in Japan', *Early Education Journal*, 72 (Spring): 6–7.

Nishida, Y. (2019), 'The Transfer, Translation and Transformation of Froebelian Theory and Practice: Annie Howe and her Glory Kindergarten and Teacher Training School in Kobe, Japan, 1889–1929', in T. Bruce, P. Elfer and S. Powell (eds), *The Routledge International Handbook of Froebel and Early Childhood Practice: Re-articulating Research and Policy*, 53–6. London: Routledge.

Nishida, Y. and F. Abe (2017), '"Come Let Us Live with Our Children": Undokai, the Children's Play Festival at the Froebelian Kindergarten in Japan, 1889–2015', in H. May, K. Nawrotzki and L. Prochner (eds), *Kindergarten Narratives on Froebelian Education: Transnational Investigations*, 151–67, London: Bloomsbury.

Opie, I. and P. Opie (1980), *The Singing Game*. Oxford: Oxford University Press.

Ouvry, M. (2001), *Exercising Muscles and Minds: Outdoor Play and the Early Years Curriculum*. London: National Early Years Network.

Ouvry, M. (2012), 'Froebel's Mother Songs Today', in T. Bruce (ed.), *Early Childhood Practice: Froebel Today*, 107–20, London: Sage.

Palmer, A. and J. Read, J. (eds) (2020), *British Froebelian Women from the Mid-nineteenth to the Twenty-first Century: A Community of Progressive Educators*. London: Routledge.

Parker, L. (n.d.), *Exploring Clay*. London: Froebel Trust.

Poulson, E. (1921), *Finger Plays for Nursery and Kindergarten,* music by C. Roeske. Norwood, MA: Norwood Press (originally printed in Boston in 1893 by Lothrop, Lee and Shepard).

Powell, S. and K. Goouch (2019), 'Mothers' Songs in Daycare for Babies', in T. Bruce, P. Elfer and S. Powell (eds), *The Routledge International Handbook of Froebel and Early Childhood Practice: Re-articulating Research and Policy,* 154–65. London: Routledge.

Powell, S. and K. Goouch with L. Werth (2012–2015), *Mothers' Songs in Daycare for Babies,* Canterbury Christ Church University Research Centre for Children, Families and Communities: Report to the Froebel Trust Research Committee.

Powell, S., K. Goouch and L. Werth (2014), 'Froebel's Mother Songs and Daycare for Babies', *Early Education Journal,* 72 (Spring): 4–5.

Prochner, L. (2017), 'Tracking Kindergarten as a Travelling Idea', in H. May, K. Nawrotzki and L. Prochner (eds), *Kindergarten Narratives on Froebelian Education: Transnational Investigations,* 1–14. London: Bloomsbury.

Prochner, L. and A. Kirova (2017), 'Kindergarten at the Dewey School, University of Chicago', in H. May, K. Nawrotzki and L. Prochner (eds), *Kindergarten Narratives on Froebelian Education: Transnational Investigations,* 99–120. London: Bloomsbury.

Ransom, J. (1997), *Foucault's Discipline.* Durham, NC: Duke University Press.

Read, J. (2012), 'The Time Honoured Tradition of Learning Out of Doors', in T. Bruce (ed.), *Early Childhood Practice: Froebel Today,* 69–80. London: Sage.

Read, J. (2017), 'Freeing the Child: Frobelians and the Transformation of Learning through Play, Self-Activity and Project Work in English Junior School Classrooms, 1917–1952', in H. May, K. Nawrotzki and L. Prochner (eds), *Kindergarten Narratives on Froebelian Education: Transnational Investigations,* 135–51, London: Bloomsbury.

Read, J. (2018), 'Taking Froebel Abroad: Transnational Travel by Froebel Teachers in the 1910s and 2010s: India and South Africa', *Early Years,* 38 (2): 156–70.

Read, J. (2019a), 'Tracing Froebel's Legacy: The Spread of the Kindergarten Movement across Europe and beyond and his Influence on Educators', in T. Bruce, P. Elfer and S. Powell (eds), *The Routledge International Handbook of Froebel and Early Childhood Practice: Re-articulating Research and Policy,* 14–18. London: Routledge.

Read, J. (2019b), 'From Gutter to Sand Pile: Discourses of Space and Place in Interventions in Working-Class Children's Play', in T. Bruce, P. Elfer and S. Powell (eds), *The Routledge International Handbook of Froebel and Early Childhood Practice: Re-articulating Research and Policy,* 264–8. London: Routledge.

Ronge, J. and B. Ronge (1855), *A Practical Guide to the English Kindergarten, (Children's Garden).* London: Hodson.

Ross, B., M. Barat and T. Fujioka (2017), 'Sound Making Actions Lead to Immediate Plastic Changes of Neuromagnetic Evoked Responses and Induced Oscillations during Perception', *Journal of Neuroscience,* 4 (1): 183–92.

Rousseau ([1762]1979), *Emile,* trans. A. Bloom. New York: Basic Books.

Scacchi, V. (2019a), 'Social and Conceptual Spaces, Froebelian Geographies: Project for the Froebel Archive Collection located at the University of Roehampton', in T. Bruce, P. Elfer and S. Powell (eds), *The Routledge International Handbook of Froebel and Early Childhood Practice: Re-articulating Research and Policy,* 46–50. London: Routledge.

Scacchi, V. (2019b) *Social and Conceptual Spaces, Froebelian Geographies: Resources for the Froebel Archive Collection Located at the University of Roehampton,* London: Froebel Trust.

Shapiro, M. (1983), *Child's Garden: The Kindergarten Movement from Froebel to Dewey.* University Park, PA: Pennsylvania State University Press.

Smith, M. (1983), 'Froebel and Religious Education', *Early Child Development and Care,* 12 (3 and 4): 303–18.

Snider, D. (1900), *Psychology of Children's Play – Gifts.* St Louis, MO: Sigma.

Solly, K. (2014), *Risk, Challenge and Adventure in Early Years.* London: Routledge.

Spratt, J. (2012), 'The Importance of Hand and Finger Rhymes: A Froebelian Approach to Early Literacy', in T. Bruce (ed.), *Early Childhood Practice: Froebel Today,* 95–106. London: Sage.

Stead, W. T. (1905), *Mother Songs and Games.* London: Books for Bairns.

Steedman, C. (1985), 'The Mother made Conscious: The Historical Development of a Primary School Pedagogy', *History Workshop Journal,* 20 (1) (October): 120–32.

Taoka, Y. (2019), 'The Educational Meaning of "Wander" in Nature According to the Development of Early Childhood', in T. Bruce, P. Elfer and S. Powell (eds), *The Routledge International Handbook of Froebel and Early Childhood Practice: Re-articulating Research and Policy,* 114–21. London: Routledge.

Tovey, H. (2012), 'Adventurous and Challenging Play Outdoors', in T. Bruce (ed.), *Early Childhood Practice: Froebel Today,* 43–56. London: Sage.

Tovey, H. (2017), *Bringing the Froebel Approach to Your Early Years Practice,* 2nd edn. London: Routledge.

Tovey, H. (n.d.), *Outdoor Play and Exploration.* London: Froebel Trust.

Tovey, H. *(forthcoming), A Froebelian Approach: Froebel's Principles and Practice Today.* London: Froebel Trust.

Trevarthen, C., J. Delafield-Butt and A. W. Dunlop (eds), *The Child's Curriculum.* Oxford: Oxford University Press.

Valkanova, Y. (2019), 'The Psychoanalytic Kindergarten Project in Soviet Russia 1921–1930', in T. Bruce, P. Elfer and S Powell (eds), *The Routledge International Handbook of Froebel and Early Childhood Practice: Re-articulating Research and Policy,* 50–3, London: Routledge.

von Marenholtz -Bulow, B. (1891), *Reminiscences of Friedrich Froebel,* trans. Mrs Horace Mann. Boston: Lee and Shepherd.

Vygotsky, L. (1978), *Mind in Society: The Development of Higher Psychological Processes.* London: Harvard University Press.

Welton, J. (1912), *Froebel: Chief Writing,* trans. S. S. F. Fletcher. London: Edward Arnold.

Weston, P. (1998), *Friedrich Froebel: His Life, Times and Significance.* London: Roehampton Institute.

Weston, P. (2002), *The Froebel Educational Institute: The Origins and History of the College.* London: University of Surrey.

Whinnett, J. (2006), 'Froebelian Practice Today: The Search for Unity', *Early Childhood Practice: The Journal for Multi-Professional Partnerships,* 8 (2): 58–79.

Whinnett, J. (2012), 'Gifts and Occupations: Froebel's Gifts (Wooden Block Play) and Occupations (Constructions and Workshop Experiences) Today', in T. Bruce (ed.), *Early Childhood Practice: Froebel Today,* 121–37, London: Sage.

Whinnett, J. (forthcoming), *A Froebelian Approach: Blockplay.* London: Froebel Trust.

Winnicott, D. W. (1974), *Playing and Reality.* Harmondsworth: Penguin.

Wright, M. and A. Albertz (eds) (2010), *Anni: Letters and Writings of Anne Marie Wachter,* Robertsbridge: Plough Publishing House of Church Communities Foundation.

INDEX